N

THE FEMINIST UTOPIA PROJECT

FIFTY-SEVEN VISIONS OF A WILDLY BETTER FUTURE

EDITED BY ALEXANDRA BRODSKY AND RACHEL KAUDER NALEBUFF

fp

THE
FEMINIST PRESS
AT THE CITY UNIVERSITY
OF NEW YORK
NEW YORK CITY

3538925

Published in 2015 by the Feminist Press
at the City University of New York
The Graduate Center
365 Fifth Avenue, Suite 5406
New York, NY 10016

feministpress.org

This book was made possible thanks to a grant from New York State Council on the Arts with the support of Governor Andrew Cuomo and the New York State Legistlature.

First printing October 2015

Cover and text design by Drew Stevens
Icons by Suki Boynton

Library of Congress Cataloging-in-Publication Data

The feminist utopia project / edited by Alexandra Brodsky and Rachel Kauder Nalebuff.
    pages cm
  Includes index.
  ISBN 978-1-55861-900-5 (pbk.) — ISBN 978-1-55861-901-2 (ebook)
  1. Feminism. 2. Utopias. 3. Feminism—Literary collections. I. Brodsky, Alexandra.
II. Kauder-Nalebuff, Rachel, editor.
  HQ1155.F4488 2015
  305.42—dc23
                                                        2015012150

For Zoe, Valerie, Ms. Gerling,
and everyone who believes
this world can be a better place.
And especially for those who don't.

Introduction

We want more.

These three simple words are so difficult to say because we, as women, aren't allowed to want much.

When we yearn for more—food, power, sex, love, time—we are gluttonous, egomaniacal, slutty, desperate, silly. To want less, to be less hungry, we are told, is to be "reasonable." After long enough, we tell ourselves this, too. Sexism justifies itself by commandeering our logic and, quietly, the limits of what *is* constrict our ideas of what *should be*. Misogyny comes to taste like air, feel like gravity: so common we barely notice it, so entrenched it's hard to conceive of a world without it.

So how can we propose new ways of living when misogyny fogs even our imaginations? And even if we tried—where and when would we organize not just to preserve what we have but to build a wildly better future?

We're in the midst of a feminist resurgence, but we still rarely find a break from today's crises to think about what we might want for tomorrow. How can we dream big when we are constantly playing whack-a-mole with the patriarchy?

These questions fueled the project that became the anthology in your hands. The fifty-seven essays, stories, poems, and artworks you hold are food for your creative feminist imagination. Our hope is that they will spark feminist dreams of your own so that we can all be ambitious, egomaniacal gluttons together.

We felt we needed this book now more than ever because it's so easy to internalize the limitations imposed on us by American electoral politics. Our hopes for progress are confined by what (usually male) politicians tell us we can and can't have: they choose the options, and our demands for anything better are dismissed as unrealistic. *Legal abortion, maybe, but no government support. Protection from pregnancy discrimination, perhaps, but your employer can treat you as badly as any other worker. Legislation to protect queer and trans people, fine, but only if it's riddled with religious exceptions.* We appeal for legal protection as discrete, insular groups—women, queers, people of color—because that is the only way government officials and courts can see us, even though our identities rarely fit into such neat boxes. To make any progress at all, we learn to play by the rules. Gendered inequality can start to feel inevitable.

When we started this project in 2012 it certainly felt that way. Alexandra had just graduated from college and was busy dealing with the disappointing aftermath of a Title IX complaint that had failed to hold her university responsible for rape. Rachel was still in school, writing a play about the slow and insidious erosion of our reproductive rights. President Obama was running for reelection, and our choices were preserving the status quo with him or moving backward with Mitt Romney, with no option for great progress. We were at the beginning of our journeys as activists, feminists, and grown-ups—and, as classmates and friends, we wondered together if the rest of our lives would be spent playing defense.

But our idealism, precisely because it was so easily dismissed, felt like it might just be our ultimate tool. We still thought things could be better. We wanted to know what that would look like. And so we started asking writers, activists, artists, and friends we admired about their visions for a feminist utopia.

The value of utopian thinking isn't uncontroversial in social justice circles. We started the project cautiously, knowing from our own organizing experiences that the quest for radical purity can come at the expense of addressing the urgent, ugly realities on the ground. We've seen activists refuse to accept imperfect solutions and end up with none, leaving the status quo just as it is in the name of change. As one of our contributors asked us, might utopian thinking devalue those who adapt their strategies—for progress and for survival—to current conditions?

The way we see it, it takes courage and ingenuity to make the compromises needed to survive, let alone improve, the current world. Waiting to act until the revolution or the formulation of a perfect fix is a luxury—and this book is certainly not about stalling activism. We recognize that, ultimately, it is people and actions that will create our better future.

For us, caring for today and tomorrow are intertwined. To build this future, we must envision it first. Even as we strategize for the realities of today, we must picture where we are headed and summon the hope to continue moving. Plus, in its own way, dreaming itself is an act of rebellion right here, right now. By simply imagining and claiming a right to a better, freer life, women reject the lives we are allowed and the people we are allowed to be.

We found that reimagining society piece by piece was the only way we could grapple with the seismic shift necessary to usher in a full-bodied utopia. In this way, each contribution charts a different corner of a utopia; collectively, they illuminate the outline of a better world. We started with specific questions: What would marriage look like? What about a constitution that was truly trans-inclusive? What would be different about birth control? About sports? Road trips? In a feminist utopia, how would we talk about sex? How would we *have* sex? What would labor industry standards designed for women be? What would feminist mental health care look like? What would a day in the life of a woman with a disability look like in a feminist utopia? What would be different for teen moms? For parents of color? For a teenage rock band? For queer love?

Answering any one of these questions requires massive structural upheavals. Madeleine Schwartz explores the intricacies and effects of a universal basic income, and Katherine Cross restructures our entire legal language and code with her sweeping feminist constitution. Even seemingly narrow changes—like collective appreciation for teen girls' speech patterns, as Katie J.M. Baker imagines in her essay—require shaking the very foundations of our world.

The collection of pieces in this book does not draw a blueprint for a single cohesive utopia. Indeed, you'll find that some of the contributions contradict each other. Many of our writers imagine the fall of sexism and capitalism together, but Sheila Bapat writes about a world where we've harnessed the potential of the latter to fight the former. Verónica Bayetti Flores imagines traditional displays of femininity as a source of strength in her story about a textile artist, while Tyler Cohen draws a schoolyard where aesthetics are freed from gender entirely.

As readers, we are interested in historical and literary utopias with flawed, realistic people organizing to care for one another. Accordingly, most of the contributions aren't set in glittery la-la lands (although Miss Major Griffin-Gracy's vision involves a lot of boogying) but in worlds where we still miscommunicate, land ourselves in hospitals, and need to put food on the table. But in these utopias, we know how to handle our human messiness. Ellen Bravo describes what an office would look like: someone still has to clean up at the end of the day, but it could be done differently. Mariame Kaba and Bianca Diaz imagine how communities could respond to (rare) instances of violence. Chloe Angyal talks about breakups that sound, well, a lot less miserable. Melissa Harris-Perry wonders if pain might exist in a utopia—if only for the sake of love. As she tenderly explains in her interview, so much of falling in love is "tied up in telling one another the stories of your struggle."

Perhaps unsurprisingly, then, visions of utopia often emerge from contributors' own experiences of hardship. Our demands are necessarily shaped by intimate knowledge of our pasts and presents. What we dream of for the future tells us about our lives today, too.

As editors, not every vision in this anthology reflects our personal utopias. And we don't expect you to agree with all of them, either. Instead, we seek to present you with a range of radically inventive thought experiments that shed the restrictions of sexist logic to spark our collective imaginations.

Our great hope for this anthology is not only that you, the reader, will finish the last page with some new insights but also that the pieces within this book will make you hungry. We hope that they will nourish but not sate, providing you with comfort, companionship, and pleasure—but also anger at how far we are from these visions. We hope this book will ignite your feminist imaginations to help you dream bigger and weirder and inspire our movements to greater collective ambitions.

There's a lot more dreaming to do. Let's dig in.

—Alexandra and Rachel

Reproductive Supporters

JUSTINE WU

My name is Mei. I have been asked to tell you about my abortion. No one has ever asked me to write something for publication before. They said I would be good for this because I can be the "voice of an ordinary woman." I'm not sure if I am supposed to be happy about that, but I guess being ordinary is good for once. They said my story will be put in a book with stories of other women, some from now and some from the past, way back before the Law.

Anyway, back to my abortion. It was pretty fast and a little bit easier than my first abortion because the second time I asked my RS (her name is Madison), "Can you please play that old song by Beyoncé so I don't have to listen to the tree sound recordings?" I got up off the bed, but then the cramps sat me right back down. Madison gave me some tea and cookies and we listened to some more music and I felt better. I asked to borrow

Madison's new Beyoncé music and she said, "Sure, just don't lose it." Then she dropped me off at home. That is pretty much it. I am not sure what else I am supposed to say. Oh, and Madison said the reason I got pregnant this time may be because my Clock (V1.3) insert was off a little (maybe I forgot to charge it?), but she adjusted it and said it should be good for a lifetime now.

Madison has been my RS since I got my period. I was twelve years old and had just filled out my Reproductive Life Plan at the Community Health Office (CHO). Just a week before, Mama was looking at my chest and saw my T-shirt was getting tight. She sat me down and said, "Mei, now that you are getting to be a woman, are you ready to talk about your Life Plan? Your sister did so around the same age, and I think it would be good if you got ready to." I just nodded and said, "Okay, Mama, no biggie," even though inside I was nervous and excited at the same time.

It was all good timing. Right after my period, the CHO assigned Madison to me because she was my sister's RS and we all got along really good. Madison knew she wanted to be a Reproductive Supporter since she was a little girl. She finished school really fast and enrolled as a Life Navigator (LN) first, but then got bored of that. She then went off to work with older women who had been Reproductive Supporters. After some time she was ready to be an RS herself.

Madison helped me with my first Clock when I was eighteen years old, just before I had sex with Leon. Right around that time, she asked, "This guy a good one?" and I said yes, and then we talked for a long time about Leon and me. She asked me if I wanted to be active with him, and I said probably and maybe we should get the Clock done. And so Madison came by the next day with the Clock (V1.2). It fit beautifully, and I sat around admiring it when nobody was looking. Like, all the time for two weeks straight. Speaking of time, the first Clock actually did show the time! I could also program in reminders for homework and stuff and download a whole mess of songs. But that was the problem—I crashed the Clock with all the data, and that is how I ended up pregnant the first time. The next Clock (V1.3) was simpler without all the extras though they are still working out the charging issues. Still, Madison thought it was good for me, and it is still working to this day.

When we were teens, Madison came by our house a lot because she was our Life Navigator too. My parents really needed the help—it was hard for them to take care of us with jobs in two different states. And they loved having Madison around to help us with English homework since they were still trying to figure out English themselves. But most of the time, we would sit around and finish English pretty quickly, and then Madison would have us teach her our language. Sometimes she would stay to cook dinner, and we would go to a movie after. We always had her over for the big holidays.

I am now twenty-nine. I never liked school and don't write that well, but Mama and Papa and Madison made me finish this. I am really good at drawing and art. So that is what I do. I sell some pictures now and then and make enough for a few months at a time. I am no longer with Leon. Now I have Ken who *is* a writer, but I did not let him touch this story. We will probably marry soon, though that is kind of old-fashioned.

Growing up, I never thought about how old Madison was, and she never told us her age. But I guessed she was born way before my Mama and Papa because she remembers things from before the Law. It is hard to know if she is telling the truth or just trying to scare us. Back then, Madison said, nobody had an RS. You had to see a doctor to get pills (that you swallowed like food!) to stop your eggs, and you had to do it every day or else you could get pregnant. And if you did get pregnant, you had to see a doctor, usually a different doctor in a different place (sometimes you had to drive really far, like over a day) if you wanted an abortion. You had to pay for the abortion yourself or your job paid. (Very strange, why should your boss care?) Some women never could get the abortion and ended up just having babies they did not want. Again, sometimes I don't know if she made stuff up to scare me and my sister into getting our Clocks. It is hard to know, but I did read about it in history class, and her version seems to be about the same as what they said in books.

Exactly ten months ago, Madison came over to pause my Clock. She asked in her matter-of-fact voice after we had eaten chicken salad sandwiches and had our tea,

"This guy a good one?" I said, "Yes, absolutely yes. He is good and he is The One." Then I looked her straight in the eye (which is hard for anyone to do, but then she knows I am serious), "I think it is time to pause. I am ready." And so it was done the next day. Before she left, Madison kissed and hugged me.

Mama just came over and asked if I was ready to feed. She nicely reminds me to be done with this story because it is late and the story has to end at some point. I said, "Okay, this is a good place to stop." Then Mama puts my baby in my arms, and I bring her close to my breast and whisper, "Time to eat, little Madison."

Justine Wu *is an abortion provider in New Jersey.*

Dispatch From the Post-Rape Future
Against Consent, Reciprocity, and Pleasure

MAYA DUSENBERY

Contents: Excerpt of an interview with one of the historians who discovered twenty-first-century American rape culture

File status: Classified

Well, at first we were just confused. Utterly confused. We were reading all these statistics from ancient government reports about the scope of the epidemic, and it was clear that the numbers were supposed to be shocking, but we couldn't really feel it at that point, you know? "One in five American women will be raped." Okay. Yikes? But we didn't know—really know—what that meant. We gathered the literal meaning soon enough. The word "rape" was obviously unfamiliar to us since it no longer exists in any present-day language. But we read the criminal codes, we read the handbooks, we got it. And still it meant amazingly little. "Forced penetration." What does that look like? "Nonconsensual sex." Nonsense. "Sexual assault." How does sex become weaponized? "Sexual violence." A contradiction in terms. It wasn't horrifying at all—just literally unimaginable.

Once we started to read the personal accounts from survivors and watch the visual depictions, the outlines became clearer. We could understand violence, of course. And power and coercion and fear. After all, it's not like our own culture is some utopia. We began to feel the appropriate horror then. Still, though, there was this nagging perplexity. We couldn't understand the silence and the shame—if this terrible thing was happening so frequently, why were so few survivors talking about it? Above all, our question was simply: "Why?" That basic question was surprisingly difficult to figure out. We sensed this underlying assumption that rape, though wrong, was somehow understandable, even inevitable, which led to a lot of resignation—and with it all these tips for "how to avoid becoming a victim" and concern about drinking and rape whistles and nail polish that detects date-rape drugs, etc. And then, on the other hand, there were the "feminists" who were deliberately refusing resignation, saying, "But, look, it doesn't have to be like this—we can change things," and demanding accountability for rapists and bystander intervention and "consent education." But, in either case, no one was really offering us very many clues about why, exactly, it was that anyone would want to rape someone.

I remember the moment I realized just how much more study it would take to make sense of this culture. I'd come across this activist campaign that proclaimed, "Consent is sexy." They had these posters and T-shirts and some very well-meaning messages. But as I was puzzling over all of it, I suddenly found myself on the verge of tears. I did not think consent was sexy in the least. These days, you'd only see the word "consent" in legal documents, right? It's about as far from "sexy" as you can get. And the thing is, that was just as true back then too. "Consent" had the same connotations of formality—as far as we could tell, the only time it was used in the realm of personal human relationships at all was in the case of sex. And, like today, it meant permission—nothing more. These posters advised men to ask their partners, "Is this okay with you?" Okay? I mean, can you imagine? No, of course you can't. Because these days, desire, not consent, is the standard. And desire can't help but make itself known. It speaks, it demands, it begs. If you have to ask, it probably isn't there. Against all logic, I found myself wondering if these people had ever actually had sex. Seriously! [Laughs] How on earth could it ever be unclear if sex was not merely "okay," as if sex were some minor inconvenience, a small favor like borrowing a toothbrush or something, but urgently wanted? That was the moment it really hit me: if the ancients were creating campaigns like this—if consent, of all things, had somehow become their rallying cry—well, there were deeper, more fundamental problems with the entire sexual culture than we had heretofore realized.

So we dove in. We studied everything that helped shape the ancients' ideas about sex—from their official sex-education programs to the unofficial messages they absorbed from films, TV shows, pop music, porn, advertising, you name it. We mined social media sites, did close readings of Facebook threads, spent days immersed in YouTube wormholes. We learned about hooking up and getting laid. About fucking and getting fucked. About hos and players and double standards. We learned that virginity was something you lost and pussy was something you scored. We learned that sex was often a zero-sum game. We learned there were rules for avoiding the label of "slut." And when we diligently tried to catalog them all, literally tallying them down in a master spreadsheet, we learned the game was rigged. We learned about shame. We learned everything we could about this odd culture of contradictions that demanded women be "sexy" and then disdained them for it; that was at once saturated in depictions of sex but very uncomfortable actually talking about it; that both celebrated and feared sexual freedom and clearly didn't know the first thing about it. I mean, you've read the report; it's quite fascinating stuff. At the end of the day, we drew some conclusions, something terribly dry and academic along the lines of: "While women were increasingly afforded a degree of sexual agency, they were still expected to play the role of sexual gatekeepers, responsible for managing how their sexuality would provoke men's sexuality, which—through a complicated interplay between gender inequality and shame around sexuality—was assumed to be inherently predatory."

Were we right? Who knows. I always say the only thing I feel confident concluding about twenty-first-century sexual culture is that it was the opposite of our own in nearly every way—and that my biggest takeaway from our research is that I'm very grateful to live in the time that I do. [*Laughs*] I'm only half joking. We don't know exactly how this culture came to be—and we don't know exactly how it changed. And we probably never will, since the records of this brief period at the beginning of the twenty-first century are the only ones that were recovered after many millennia of history were lost in the Great Crash. But we're living proof that eventually—and you even see the beginnings of the shift starting during the Ancient Era—the culture was transformed so radically that rape is as unthinkable today as it was normalized back then. And we recommended that the report be sealed to the general public because that's how it should stay; to borrow a phrase from the ancients, some ideas are best left to "the ash heap of history."

And what's remarkable is just how thoroughly it has been. I mean, just look at the language. Although the term "sex" is still used in scientific contexts today, our colloquial word is derived from the twenty-first-century words "empathy" and "ecstasy"—translated to ancient English, it means "to feel the pleasure that another feels." Imagine the ancients trying to wrap their heads around that! For one thing, they seemed to be partial to euphemisms for sex that obscured rather than revealed anything real about it. So directly acknowledging pleasure would probably have embarrassed them. And the notion that each partner's pleasure might actually be dependent on the other's, that this might be inherent in the very definition of sex, well, that upends their most deep-seated assumptions about sexuality. Bizarre as it sounds to you and me, they truly seemed to believe that, free of any social constraints, sexuality was naturally selfish and exploitative.

This dismal view meant they were nearly incapable of imagining sex without a subject-object dynamic. Traditionally, of course, this was a male aggressor and female gatekeeper. He initiates, she consents. He fucks, she is fucked. He takes, she gives. Clearly, these models were rooted in inequality between the genders and relied on a sexist myth that autonomous female desire simply didn't exist. But by the twenty-first century, the feminist movement had made a great many gains and had mostly put that myth to rest. To be sure, there was still resistance to women's sexual agency—as evidenced by the rampant victim blaming and "slut shaming" that marked the era. But it seemed to be driven in part by a larger fear of sexual freedom. After all, if you believe that unfettered sexuality is destructive and suddenly women are claiming a right to sexual agency and abdicating their traditional role as sexual gatekeepers—well, it's going to provoke a lot of anxiety.

Still, the growing equality between the genders required these old sexual models to be tweaked. But they didn't change much—the only difference was that now sex was imagined as mutually exploitative. Now women, too, could fuck—not just be fucked. In the most "equal" of sexual relationships, ideally both partners would "enthusiastically consent" to be both subject and object. They used one another as an instrument of their own sexual pleasure just as much as they were used in return. But since the idea of men as sexual objects still made the ancients uncomfortable, once it became a two-way street, the subject-object model largely gave way to a transactional one. Sex could now be imagined as a fair "tit-for-tat" trade of sexual pleasure between equals— an almost economic exchange in which "reciprocity" was valued. (The ancients, remember, were some of the last capitalists.) Measured strictly in terms of gender equality, this shift, which at least acknowledged that men and women are equally sexual beings, was certainly an improvement. But it didn't fundamentally alter their pessimistic conception of sexuality at all. Because of that, while the ancients hoped such reciprocity could be guaranteed by a sense of fairness, they didn't really expect it to be. Only a committed relationship was believed to provide the motivation to reciprocate.

Contrast this with our sexual model. For us, desire feeds desire in such an instantaneous and continual positive feedback loop that the line between object and subject becomes hopelessly blurred. I want you because you want me because I want you because you want me. The idea that sex could happen without this mutual desire driving it is beyond comprehension. Not, as the ancients liked to admonish, out of "respect" for our partner or for some legalistic definition of consent but simply because desire attracts desire, like two magnets drawn closer and closer together, and if the charge goes out of either, [*snaps fingers*] the pull that had been so inexorable and undeniable is broken and both tumble apart. And reciprocity! [*Waves hand in disdain*] Reciprocity has nothing to do with it. We don't give our partners pleasure so that they give us pleasure in return. The mutuality in our sex is not based on something as abstract as fairness or contingent on something as rare as commitment. If you are literally "feeling the pleasure that another feels," it's simply impossible to say where your pleasure starts and the other's begins. It certainly couldn't be parceled up to be exchanged. Selfishly hoarding it is self-defeating. And actually inflicting pain would be a crime against yourself, as well.

So you can see how the ancients' conception of sex as

naturally exploitative made rape an ever-present possibility, while ours makes it difficult to imagine. But their problems also stemmed from the fact that they had no real understanding of sex as important beyond itself. They were really quite confused about the point of it. For some, it was strictly about procreation, and so sex was an indulgence at best, immoral at worst. For others, it was an expression of love—but it was the love that was exalted, considered worthy of celebration and cultural approval. Sex was permitted as just one of many ways of expressing it. By the twenty-first century, those who believed sex was a natural human desire outside of these narrowly prescribed contexts had begun to claim sexual pleasure, in and of itself, as the point. The broader culture, long caught between its puritanical roots and consumerist excesses, was typically contradictory, alternating between embracing the banner of pleasure and decrying such superficial hedonism. And all this was happening in the midst of an ongoing, but not yet complete, breakdown of gender inequality. So for women, whose sexual desire had been repressed until that point, sex was often also about empowerment—about claiming a right to pleasure and agency long denied them. And, of course, sex also became yet another—quite frightening— realm of patriarchal backlash, as men used it to assert power they felt rapidly slipping away from them.

As you can imagine, all this made the conversation about the meaning of sex quite confusing. By the end of the era, "pleasure" had largely won the battle, but there was a sense that it wasn't quite up for the job. For example, the ancients had this tendency to say, "It's just sex." What a strange way of belittling sex, while simultaneously claiming their right to it. The way they used that short phrase spoke volumes about how they considered sexuality to be hopelessly disconnected from, and in fact often at odds with, all those things they aspired to most. It drew a line between sex and love, between the physical and the emotional, between mere pleasure and something more. Trapped in such false dichotomies, and having rejected the idea that sex had to mean everything, they began to dismiss it as nothing at all.

Sex, to us, is both more and less serious than it seemed to be to the ancients. They were right, of course, in suspecting that pleasure, per se, makes for a rather flimsy purpose for sex. Pleasure is lovely, yes, and the ancients would have done well to treat the pursuit of it, in countless spheres of their lives, with the importance it deserves. But once one's own sexuality is known, pleasure is always, quite literally, at the tip of your fingers. No, the point of sex is knowledge. Knowledge of another's sexuality, knowledge of ourselves in relation to them, knowledge of the unique alchemy that happens in the space where two individuals' desire meets. This knowledge—the kind gained by stepping outside yourself, the kind that changes you—is, of course, our highest value, the very foundation on which our society is built. While the ancients didn't seem to have a word for it, there were hints that they, too, longed for such knowledge. Their individualistic culture couldn't completely repress this innate desire to expand—to erase the boundaries between ourselves and the world and everything in it. We can only guess, but perhaps the culture began to change once they stopped seeing sexuality as at odds with this project and recognized that, in fact, sex can be our greatest teacher. I just hope this transformation happened in time for some of the ancients to experience empatextas.

Maya Dusenbery *is the editorial director of* Feministing. *She lives, writes, and thinks about sex in Atlanta, Georgia.*

Dispatches from a Body Perfect World

JENNY TROUT

Forty New 3-D Garment Printers Employed at Midtown Clothing Depot
January 26, 2801
Ames, Fourth Sector

The Clothing Depot located in the midtown sector has announced plans to update its garment printing software and install forty new, state-of-the-art 3-D garment printers as early as this spring. The machines will allow citizens to simply scan their body shapes, rather than requiring them to enter their measurements manually.

Clothing Depot head officer Gail Shaikh assures customers that the overall process of selection and checkout will remain the same. "You'll still go to the dress section or the shirt section, get your item number, try out the look on the holomodel. That part will all be the same." Shaikh says the garment construction and printing stage will face the most changes. "You'll still enter the style number, but the optical intelligence sensors will scan you and size the garment appropriately."

Says Shaikh, "The problem is that most people don't measure themselves, so when it comes time to buy clothes, they end up with pieces that aren't perfectly tailored to their particular shape. That will all change with the new printers." The Protectorate hopes this will reduce the wait time for citizens and lessen the amount of waste due to user error.

New Holoplay Examines the Severity of Ancient Body Beliefs

February 8, 2801
Detroit, Seventh Sector

Imagine an era where citizens are so concerned with the size and shape of their bodies that the obsession drives the sales of everything from exercise equipment to books, even surgery. *Shrink*, a new holoplay from acclaimed director Amanda Acai, brings this fascinating culture to life, following the stories of four woman-identifying, twenty-first-century humans.

"The interesting thing we see in ancient literature is the theme of fear of aging. These people didn't seem to fear the ends of their lives as much as they dreaded non-medical effects of aging." Acai says these women were "doing everything in their power to avoid loose upper arms, lines on their faces."

Some, such as acclaimed performer Rose Sena's character, Charlotte, resorted to surgical modifications to escape the relentless pressure of ancient society. "This was such a cruel time because this wasn't a choice they made freely, like the modifications of today. This was an expectation, that women would not age."

The holoplay will air Wednesday, August 5, at 20:00 on Historiogram.

Relics of the Fourth Dark Age Arrive at Twelfth Sector Museum
May 24, 2801
New Haven, Twelfth Sector

Ancient relics from Earth's Fourth Dark Age arrived at a history museum in the Twelfth Sector today. Curator Rhonda Warburton describes the collection as a peek into a time archaeologists are just beginning to understand.

"This is a picture of an era that is so different to what we know now. I think it will surprise, and frankly shock, a lot of people."

The exhibit puts some six hundred objects on display.

From two-dimensional image screens to a rudimentary stim-brewing device known as a "Mr. Coffee," the artifacts paint a clearer picture of how ancient humans lived.

"We see a difference in costume. Their clothing was gendered, and it appears to have followed some caste system." Warburton says that those with smaller bodies were given smaller clothing, with less protection from the elements. "There is some debate in the archeological community over whether this is a sign that these people with thinner bodies were lower-class citizens or if our earlier beliefs about the emphasis on body weight in their culture were too extreme."

Among these household items on display are body-modification devices such as scales that measured weight and nonbiodegradable packaging from nutritionally devoid food. Warburton says citizens viewing the exhibit may recognize the contributions of ancient man to our modern world: "Certainly, when you look at the way their food was labeled and the nutritional information they were struggling to impart, it's very similar to our current system. Of course, ours is based on individual genetic makeup, but the foundation is there. This primitive people's cultish devotion to the ideal form gave us nutritional science, and we can't overlook that contribution lightly."

The Twelfth Sector Museum of Human History is open 08:00 to 03:00 Saturdays and Sundays, 11:00 to 22:00 Monday through Friday.

Last Human Bearing the "Vanity Gene" Has Died

June 1, 2801
Seattle, Ninth Sector

Harley Boye, the last known human to bear the "Vanity Gene," has died of natural causes at age 217. The gene, known to scientists as Narcissus Ioci, caused mass global strife before researchers isolated it in the year 2779. Retroepigeneticists were able to immunize the public against the effects, but Boye was one of the hundreds whose genetic makeup could not be altered. A 2790 film documented the challenges faced by these individuals, such as obsessive removal of body hair, insistence on assigning gender to clothing and cosmetics, and modifying their natural shapes with restrictive garments.

Says one caregiver, "She constantly worried that she was getting fat but couldn't explain what that meant. She expected us to, I don't know, almost instinctively know what she was talking about. It was very sad, very difficult to understand."

Funeral services will be held at the Twelfth Street memorial tree nursery. Boye's memory tree will be transferred to the Sector Six municipal park in the spring. Boye's child, Reginald Anderson, said he hoped that his mother's legacy would "not be a memory of her illness but a reminder that we should be thankful every day that science has given us such a valuable gift."

Model Returns to the Catwalk After Protectorate-Endorsed Parental Leave

October 12, 2801
San Francisco, Ninth Sector

Model Ivana Carera, a woman-identifying citizen from Sector Nine, made her much-anticipated return to the runway this week after a year of Protectorate-Endorsed Parental Leave upon the birth of her second child.

"I was so happy to return to work," Carera stated, adding, "I fully support a citizen taking the full five-year leave offered by the Protectorate, but I was getting a bit bored at home."

Carera, forty-two, walked for Ennis Swimwear.

Jenny Trout *is a blogger and* USA Today *bestselling author. She is a proud Michigander, mother of two, and wife to the only person alive capable of tolerating her for extended periods of time. Visit her blog at jennytrout.com.*

My Own Sound

CHRISTINE SUN KIM

My cousin once told me that I behaved as if I had lived my whole life in another country with their customs and rules. I was born profoundly deaf, although I have grown accustomed to the way people behave around sound. When I consider how much negotiating I do on a daily basis, I start to think that he's right. And I would like that to change. I would like to feel like I'm in a country of my own.

The nature of making sound is overtly political, after all. I can imagine a place where people are entitled to their own bodily sounds—a world in which we produce the sounds we like, when we like. No one in a fancy restaurant would give me looks when I make self-noises. Our bodies and our bodily sounds would be out and open, and they would be free of judgment.

In my feminist utopia, we could refrain from noise when that feels right, too. In this world, quietness—

which we so often associate with effeminate meek-
ness—would no longer equate vulnerability; emphasis
and volume would not be intertwined. In the past, I have
had to shout while signing to get my point across. Why
should I have to produce a sound to be taken seriously,
to show that I mean what I'm saying? As a woman this is
so complicated: I have to make sound to be recognized,
but if I make too much, I am insufficiently ladylike and
so shunned again. In this better world, I could express
myself aurally in the way that feels right for me.

In my feminist utopia, my own language would be
good enough. Sound normativity would disappear and
no one from the deaf community would need to conform to a kind of body that will never be like our own.
No one would expect us to say other people's names out
loud for the sake of that person's ego. We wouldn't feel
the need to imitate people's reactions to sound in order
to fit in. I often catch myself in lecture halls, when there
appears to be audio feedback, suddenly covering my ears
like everyone else out of some form of politeness. In my
utopia, when I sense audio feedback or a shrill tone in
the air, I wouldn't feel embarrassed by my difference. I
would feel impenetrable.

I'm envisioning a place where society values the way
each person lives and communicates. Our access to education, quality of life, and employment opportunities
would be based on the concept of "universal design"—a
set of principles enabling people with various bodies and
backgrounds to experience the world without barriers.

In my feminist utopia, the myth of a normal body would be abolished. All those access departments and special-education programs at institutions would not exist as separate, stigmatized "accommodations," but would be fully integrated. We wouldn't even need the term "universal design" because, in my utopia, the drive to build a world for all bodies wouldn't need a special term. It would just be life.

Christine Sun Kim *is a visual and sound artist whose work has been exhibited internationally and, most recently, at the Museum of Modern Art in New York City.*

A List of Thirty-Three Beautiful Things to Wear on Your Breasts

SARAH MATTHES

Since the revolution, the editorial staff at *Buzzfeed* has revisited our previously published material, including "51 Impossibly Beautiful Bras for Girls with Small Boobs"—one of our many pieces which, we are ashamed to admit, promoted capitalism and body normativity under the guise of liberation. For that, we sincerely apologize. Below is our new list of impossibly beautiful things to wear on your breast or breasts:

1. The cover of your favorite book
2. The tassel of your graduation cap
3. Two CDs hung perfectly on your nipples
4. A pair of grommets hung just the same
5. A flat bicycle tire, little grease on your cheek
6. A mystery flavor Dum Dum and a Band-Aid
7. The two plastic flames of your Lego dragon

8. The wide eye of a sunflower pressed against you in a field
9. Two elegantly constructed mud pies
10. Lenses popped from an old pair of glasses
11. A clay sculpture of King Tutankhamen your father helped you paint blue and gold
12. The first tampon you ever got successfully into and out of your body
13. A harvest moon
14. A supermoon
15. A cut-open, stinking, moist wrist cast
16. The yarmulke of a bar mitzvah boy you once kissed behind the DJ booth
17. A piece of two-by-four
18. Kindling fresh cut with your new hatchet
19. A fanny pack; you love it
20. One beer bottle and one wine cork
21. A mackerel still shaking on the lure
22. Two tea lights just snuffed out
23. The favorite page of your dissertation
24. A note you wrote when you were six with the spelling all wrong
25. Your first pay stub
26. A Gerber pocketknife

27. Some scabs
28. A wicker basket inside you once, you can't believe it
29. Your own hands
30. Your lover's hands
31. Your lover's mouth
32. A telephone receiver with your lover's voice on the other end
33. The love of yourself

Sarah Matthes *is a poet and tall-ship sailor. She lives in Berkeley, California.*

Our Bodies, Us

ELIZABETH DEUTSCH

When I had an eating disorder, I thought of myself as a brain in a formaldehyde jar. Maybe in my mind's eye the whole thing was hooked up to electrodes; it looked like a science experiment of some kind. My body was everything—the only thing I thought about. And also nothing—an incidental receptacle.

When I started getting sick, my ribs began to show like keys on a xylophone. They first showed up by my collarbone and then extended down my torso. My rings fell off my fingers. Once, I went to a club and there was lots of bass in the music and I looked down at my legs and I remember thinking, "This is very odd. Those aren't my legs." After I had been sick, I walked around my college campus and noticed, for the first time, other women struggling. I looked at them and thought, "They are all trying to borrow bodies."

I want the image that the media portrays, the women we see in ads, to stop borrowing. Stop borrowing from stick figures and Barbies. The idea of borrowed bodies is enabled by a kind of separation we imagine between our bodies and us: that the soul—the self—is separate or severable from the body. Only where there is this distance between the body and the self is the body something that should be controlled (by a fad diet, abstinence, or a pair of Spanx). Control, at its most extreme forms, means the body isn't even yours anymore.

But we should imagine bodies to be *us*. The metaphorical heart is a muscular fist that sits in a real rib cage. Being our bodies means that we can move through the world connected and whole in ourselves.

That kind of wholeness means that we don't need to be all the beautiful things we see. Imagine a world where we can enjoy beauty without needing to be it, or morphing and molding ourselves to resemble it. We could enjoy flipping through a fashion magazine on the subway ride to work and the pictures wouldn't make us want to change ourselves. Bodies in ads and mannequins in store windows would be all different shapes. Perfection wouldn't have to be zero-sum or singular. Recognizing why an angle is beautiful helps us understand why a curve is, too.

In this world, we rejoice in taking up space. Numbers on the waistbands of our jeans are different from one another without designating your rank or value. Sizes are like musical notes on a scale. Feasting, running, and dancing are all forms of learning: taking in what is around us.

I imagine returning to that club, this time feeling the vibrations of the bass with my whole self. The floor pulsates, reverberating even in my legs' tiniest tendons. Watching the lights flash and the people move, losing control isn't scary.

Elizabeth Deutsch's *writing has been published in the* New York Times, Politico *magazine, and* Bloomberg View. *She holds an MSc in gender from the London School of Economics.*

Dispatch from Outside the Girl Talk Incubator

KATIE J.M. BAKER

Like, Listen Up
July 27, 2143
New York, NY

The twelve- to fifteen-year-old girls have convened, as they do every spring, to discuss next year's vocal trends. The world waits silently—literally silently, since under Girl Talk protocol, no one is allowed to speak while the teens are assembled—to hear their forthcoming statement on the Linguistic Situation.

It, like, wasn't always this way? Once, not so long ago, a low, growling "vocal fry" was considered a disorder that made the speaker appear insecure instead of a useful tool for building relationships, as studies have long shown. Those who spoke in high-pitched, bubbly voices were discriminated against in the workplace and political office for not sounding "serious" enough. Back then, "uptalk" signified stupidity instead of sophistication, and "like" was a ditzy conversation filler instead of a conscientious discourse marker used by speakers deemed "thoughtful" and "aware of themselves and their surroundings" by personality tests.

Teenage girls' voices were considered excessively girly and copycat conformist, even though sociolinguists wrote paper after paper proving that teenage girls were half a generation ahead of males when it came to speech patterns. (Note: It was once considered disadvantageous to be excessively "girly," although now, of course, it is a high compliment that implies greater-than-average intellectual capacities.) Teenage girls were not recognized as linguistic innovators.

But they are today. All of that disrespect and incomprehension ended after the revolution and subsequent purge that, sadly, killed all the adults whose ears refused to register Girl Talk as the most empathetic and productive way to communicate.

It's, like, inconceivable that teenage girls, the most sought-after marketing demographic ever, held so much power but were ridiculed for their innovation. But that was long ago! So, like, whatever.

Katie J.M. Baker *is a reporter who has been told on more than one occasion that she sounds like a Valley Girl.*

Interview with Jessica Luther

The following is excerpted from an interview an editor conducted over the phone on August 19, 2014, with Jessica Luther, an Austin-based activist and sports critic who writes on the intersections of gender and athletics. Luther's writing has been published by Sports on Earth, the Texas Observer, *the* Austin Chronicle, *the* Atlantic, *and the* Nation. *She is currently working on a book about college football and sexual assault for Akashic Books.*

Tell us a bit about what athletic events would look like in a feminist utopia. How would things change on the field?

We would have to start with the way we handle athletics when children are young. Today, if a girl grows up playing baseball, like thirteen-year-old Mo'ne Davis, there's a point when she will be told "If you want to continue you will play softball with the girls." And there will be no resources available for her to continue playing baseball.

I like to imagine: What would Brittney Griner, a basketball player for the Pheonix Mercury, look like in utopia? Where would she be playing ball if she had been allowed or encouraged to play at the level that she was capable of playing her entire life? What if she'd never been asked to stop playing with players at her level and asked to join whatever girl's team was available? If sports were about actual athletic ability and not gender, it would revolutionize how sports function.

It's funny—this is one of the few areas where even feminists are comfortable relying on biological difference to separate young boys and girls or men and women. How would you respond to the concern that if we don't separate by sex in the utopia and just separate by ability, women will never have opportunities to play at all, or will end up at the bottom of the heap?

If we were in a utopia, where women would receive the same resources and experiences as men throughout their sporting careers, we would see women playing sports at the highest level. We would see Olympic gold medalist soccer player Abby Wambach playing with the boys if she had been given the same coaches and opportunities as men like US Olympic soccer player Landon Donovan. I don't even doubt that.

At the start there's probably going to be fewer women and girls. But that also comes from confidence. It means something to young women to see older women playing at the level that they can. It inspires them—it's all so connected. The idea that women would be picked last, at the bottom of the heap, comes from a real place. It's not necessarily a wrong prediction, but it's really all this outside stuff, it's people's beliefs about girls' abilities, not their actual abilities.

And this is particularly true for a sport like soccer—all kinds of body types are good at soccer. But even for a game like football, the idea that a woman can't go out on the field and be a quarterback when there are already so many women in this country who play football is wrong. And we already have tiny running backs; for a woman to be a running back, she'd have to be fast and gain some muscle, but women can do that.

How would a fan's experience change if there were both men and women on the field categorized by skill rather than gender?

Straight up, there would be more women in the stands. And any time you start to get crowds of people who are not all the same, things change. Certainly, I think that if we had this utopia where Abby Wambach is playing soccer for the genderless US national team we would see a change in audience demographics. Women like sports for the same reasons men do. In my utopia, there would be more gender diversity on the field in games and that would affect who shows up.

We can look at who goes to WNBA games: lots of women. People like to see themselves. This is a known cultural phenomenon: people vote for people like them. This is why diversity in media is so important.

The more women are involved, from fans to media to people who own the leagues to people who play on the teams, the more we can celebrate sports as majestic athleticism, team-building, and opportunity to commune socially rather than as a way of confirming toxic masculinity. Sports can be an arbiter for masculinity. How well you do determines how masculine you are. And there are so many things embedded in being masculine that are detrimental to both men and women, from domestic violence to sexual assault. If there were more women involved, it wouldn't be so easy to have this "look how masculine you are" contest.

I'm thinking about football: it's probably the most masculine of our sports and the most popular. There's concern right now about concussions in football, whether people should tackle less in practice, and whether certain types of hits should be illegal in order to minimize brain damage. And there's huge pushback against any regulations because people fear it will feminize the game. The whole game is propped up on this idea that it's good when you get hurt because it shows you're a man. This game is literally destroying people's brains. Players accept a lot of damage to their bodies that's justified in the language around football. Players are told: "Be a man," "This is what men do," "Men hit hard and go hard."

We demand these huge men be aggressive on the field, so how can we be surprised when off the field they continue to be physically violent? Ray Rice of the Baltimore Ravens is a particularly well-known example: he was videotaped knocking out his girlfriend and then dragging her, unconscious, out of an elevator. He pled out, even though it's pretty clear he beat her up to the point of being unconscious. People were upset about his behavior, but they also joked about it. At first he was only suspended by the league for two games, which is nothing. The NFL is a horrible league that exploits the bodies of these players and asks them to "be men" and be aggressive on the field—and then the league does nothing when they're off the field and hurt people. That kind of sanctioning is dangerous.

I hear you talking about the values that seep off the field into the larger culture. In the utopia, where Abby Wambach's granddaughter is the star player of the US multi-gender team, it seems like it would be harder to conflate athleticism and masculinity. What values do you think utopian sports would promote that would be productive?

I write a lot about sports and sexual assault, and sometimes I'll ask: "What are we getting out of these spaces? These are dangerous spaces for women. What are the takeaways, particularly with football?" And people inevitably say: team. To be supported by people, to learn from people. In an ideal world, I see that. I played basketball; I know what a team feels like. If we could strip out the sexist element, people could really benefit from that group experience. Being part of a team is a positive thing. I want people to have access to that kind of personal support.

I'm thinking about the adjectives people would use to talk about star players when that team experience was centralized: "She's such a great collaborator." I love the idea of the six-year-old watching a game on TV, internalizing those values, and thinking, "Yeah! When I grow up I'm gonna be the most supportive friend ever."

Right. And one of the ways that gets muddied right now is that people support Ray Rice because he is part of their "team" even though he beat this woman. The support language gets appropriated. People always do bad stuff, even in utopia, but in a better world we wouldn't put the sense of team loyalty above a larger sense of justice. It would be great for the word "team" to be about positive community rather than protection from responsibility.

This makes me think about bystander intervention, getting people to take responsibility for stopping sexual violence. Communities can be terrible sites of abuse because people often rally around their members no matter what they do. But you also have shared values and shared concerns. Teams, whether we're understanding them as athletic teams or communities working toward shared goals, can also decide how to hold each other accountable, so it's about value-driven commitment rather than blind support.

That's part of why gender integration is so important. If there were women in management, coaching, and playing on the field for the Baltimore Ravens, we wouldn't have all this violence from players like Ray Rice, or, at the least, the reactions to that violence would look very different. It's one thing to have to answer to the fans, but having women in the locker room talking through team standards and behavior would fundamentally change that conversation.

Right. Because even if you're just blindly loyal to your team, if your team includes people of different identities and backgrounds and experiences, you'll have to do some grappling with ethics and justice to figure out what loyalty to the groups' interest as a whole really looks like.

That's why so many organizations are working to help athletes who want to come out. If Michael Sam can play in the NFL, then what's your excuse for homophobia? Sports can lead in these moments. We think teams that are friendly to gay athletes won't only help those particular athletes, but the effect will ripple out to support other queer people. And I think it could do the same with gender parity.

One of the things that we have been talking about a lot as we edit this book is the work of utopia. We're talking about a world where we've eradicated misogyny, but with the assumption that maintaining progress takes work. I like the idea of athletic culture and sports as institutions that desperately need fixing in their own right but also could serve to preserve feminist values once we get to the utopia.

I like that. I'm a fan who is also a feminist. I like to watch sports. I get that there are people who don't, and that's fine. But there's no way to argue that sports don't play an important role in our culture. In a feminist utopia, where gender parity is a reality, where the industry isn't built on the backs of exploited bodies, we could finally experience the great things about sports, which could tell us very different stories about people and bodies than they do today.

Interview with Melissa Harris-Perry

The following is excerpted from an interview an editor conducted over the phone with professor, critic, author, and television host Melissa Harris-Perry on September 10, 2013. Harris-Perry—or "MHP" as many fans affectionately call her—is the host of the Melissa Harris-Perry show on MSNBC. At the time of the interview, Harris-Perry was a professor at Tulane University in New Orleans. As of 2014, Harris-Perry is the Presidential Endowed Chair in Politics and International Affairs at Wake Forest University, founding director of the Anna Julia Cooper Center on Gender, Race, and Politics in the South, and executive director of the Pro Humanitate Institute. In preparation for the interview, Harris-Perry mentioned she wanted to use Martin Luther King Jr.'s "I've Been to the Mountaintop" speech, in which he imagines a better future for mankind, as a starting point for reflecting on feminist progress.

I just read the "I've Been to the Mountaintop" speech for the first time. I don't think I would have noticed, unless you pointed it out, that King doesn't actually describe what the "Promised Land" of the future looks like.

In what we commonly refer to as the "I Have A Dream" speech, King fully articulates his dream in this speech—he gives us a sense of his vision for a racially just future and outlines many aspects of fully integrated life. As a result, we tend to think that when Dr. King said he'd been to the mountaintop and that he'd seen the Promised Land, the Promised Land looked like the dream he had articulated five years earlier.

But King doesn't say that. He doesn't tell us what the Promised Land looks like. It is clear from his words that King is keenly aware of the existential crisis facing him. He knows that his death is imminent—his choice *not* to outline his prophetic vision and *not* to tell us what it is that he saw feels like a meaningful choice—and one that is about reserving for us our ability to craft our own utopia.

There are a few ways to read this. We can believe that King was quite literally with God that night and God made King a deal: he could see the Promised Land, but he wasn't allowed to share the vision. Another, less literal, interpretation is that King recognizes he can't tell us what the future looks like because he's very aware of how much can and will change before we enter this new land. I assume that the Promised Land is more just and more equal than even most radical-minded 1960s activists could have imagined or grasped. Say, for example, that King's vision included gay men and women as completely equal. That's not something he could have said from the pulpit that night without sounding delusional to most people who were listening. LGBT equality wasn't even part of the political discourse for many of those civil rights activists. Whatever the reason, King left the Promised Land vision open, and it gives us a lot of room to pick up where he left off.

So what would our Promised Land, our utopia, look like? For me, feminism is less about any specific set of policies and much more about a method for doing politics and asking questions. It's holding oneself accountable to ask one question over and over again—and that question is: What truth or truths are missing here? Whenever you're engaged in a claim, like, "black people deserve civil rights"—and that's a claim that I think is a truth—you still have to ask what truths are missing. In addition to black people having full civil rights, I also believe that people of all ages deserve full human rights. I also believe that in order to talk about human rights, you have to go beyond the nation-state and talk about government and the basic rights that should be obtained no matter what regime is governing. The feminist method is a way of understanding that a thing can be true, but that its truth is typically only partial. Feminists push to find the missing truths.

Take Betty Friedan's *The Feminine Mystique*—there's a lot of truth in that book. But there's also a great deal missing for women who are not middle class, who are not white, who have found as much inequality and unfairness in the workforce as on the home front—these are just some of the truths that are missing. And that for me is the utopia project—it's to keep pushing the feminist question of what truths are missing, who's *not* sitting at the table, whose concerns are *not* being articulated, whose interests aren't being represented, and whose truths aren't being told or acknowledged.

What are some of those specific truths that we're missing that you'd want to see in your utopia?

This is hard because my utopia continues to involve struggle and discontent. This is the lesson of the movie *The Matrix*, when they ponder the question of why the machines did not simply craft a perfect world for the humans to experience. After all, remember that in *The Matrix* people are simply plugged into a machine. Our life experiences are simulated. So why not make them perfect? Why is there still suffering in the simulation? The movie offers the interesting answer that people would know it was wrong, and they'd wake up from the Matrix. A world in which nothing is wrong and there is no struggle is not a compelling human existence and isn't particularly fulfilling. My utopia would need to include struggle because it's part of what it means to be human. And struggle can be productive. I am a runner. I create struggle where there is none naturally by taking on the physical challenge of running daily. The result is a stronger body than if I avoided that struggle. We have to do things that are hard to feel fully human, to feel we have accomplished and that we have achieved. But in my utopia, the struggles we would experience would be more fundamental to our humanity and less tied to the accidental identities that we are assigned at birth.

I have a daughter—and she's an emotional person; she's a sensitive soul. She suffers in this world because criticism hurts her more than people who are less sensitive. She experiences failures and criticism as deeply emotional experiences. And I'm okay with that. That is how she is wired. That is who she is. And having an experience of struggle *that* way feels very human to me. What *isn't* reasonable is when she experiences hardship because of who she is—a little black girl. In my utopia, she would not be more likely to encounter rape and sexual assault, or more discrimination, or to have people see her as less intelligent than she is. In my utopia, she would not have to overcome a set of stereotypes that will sexualize her in her adolescence. Those things are not about who she is; they are about those identities that she was assigned at birth. For me, a feminist utopia is the time when our struggles, our anxieties, our challenges to overcome are based on our human condition and not on our identity.

That's beautiful. None of the other submissions we've gotten so far have talked about the importance of struggle, but I think you're absolutely right—that's where discourse and art and culture and personality come from. What a brilliant way of framing it.

I think about falling in love with my husband, and part of falling in love with James—and this is true for all intimate relationships whether or not they're romantic—so much of those early conversations of getting to know someone are tied up in telling one another the stories of your struggle, the things you've overcome, the difficulties and the challenges. I mean I guess we could talk about, "this time I went skiing," but . . .

That would be so boring.

Indeed! That said, I am comfortable with one period of life being relatively boring. As much as I believe in struggle, I also believe in protecting the relative autonomy and safety of childhood. I'm most disturbed by how the evils of racism and sexism distort the experience of childhood. In part, this is because I have been thinking a great deal about the fiftieth anniversary of the

bombing of the church in Birmingham. I am still emotionally devastated by the reality of those four little girls
dying as martyrs. Maybe it's because I recently had to
cover the chemical weapons attack in Syria. Maybe it's
because the letter we wrote this week on the *MHP* show
was written to a little girl in Oklahoma who was sent out
of her school for wearing dreadlocks. If MSNBC told me
I had to change my hair, it'd be racist and sexist, but I
could handle it because I'm an adult. I feel like I've been
encountering a lot of childhood suffering and it makes
me really sad. I would absolutely preserve struggle in my
utopia, but I would also want to protect childhood.

**Do you have any specific images or details for what
would happen in your utopia and the ways in which it
would be different from our world?**

Sometimes people offer the vision of a "post-racial"
world as one that is ideal. I think a world without race is
not desirable. It does *not* sound like a utopia to me! But
a world without rape does. That sounds like a utopia that
I'm willing to imagine and to think very carefully about
how to create. My feminist utopia would include a world
where whatever struggles people experience, they are
not associated with overcoming sexual violence.

**And what would change if sexual violence didn't
exist—even on a daily basis, or in a mundane way?**

In a really mundane way, I think it creates freedom of movement for women's bodies that would revolutionize the entire political and economic system in ways that are probably hard to imagine.

I don't really know what happens if women aren't afraid to go outside, anywhere, at any time of the day. One of the great privileges of manhood is the freedom of being able to walk through public space without fearing violence. And of course this is a statement about relatively privileged manhood—you know African American boys living in my neighborhood in New Orleans certainly don't feel they can be out at any time of day or night. They also fear violence—not sexual violence, but another kind of violence. And we can see very easily how much that fear shapes who they are as people and, therefore, how much it shapes our political and social economic world. We can see what happens when a group of people is afraid for their public safety. We can see it for these young boys. We see what it does to them psychologically.

It's harder for us to see it with women because it's *so* embedded in the culture. I mean, a comparison point for little black boys is that we can see grown white men who feel free . . . I mean, I don't think Donald Trump ever feels afraid outside at night. But even if you are a woman of great privilege—say my white, wealthy female students at Tulane University—any girl at this university is thinking about her bodily safety. And since she's thinking about that, I don't know what she's *not* thinking about as a result. Maybe she's not thinking about her economics homework. Or she's not going to the concert where she might have encountered a kind of music that would alter the way she makes movies someday. It could be trivial. It could be huge! But I do know that the time and energy and space women take up thinking about safety and our bodily integrity from childhood forward must take away brain energy from other things we could be doing.

Feminist Constitution

KATHERINE CROSS
ILLUSTRATION BY RUTH TAM

Preamble

What if, instead of being mummified by lofty obscurity, law lived up to its potential? Law, after all, defines our obligations to one another and establishes that lattice-work of mutual bonds that connect us as citizens and unite us through our highest principles. Law grants utterance to our collective priorities, our aspirations, our hopes, and our realities; it bespeaks the society we wish to be. We are the law, and the law is us. Constitutions are the marble foundation of such laws, the ultimate list of priorities, in a sense. They are composed of a given society's red lines and safe words. At their best, they guide a nation toward its dreams. Yet America's constitution has had little to no input from women or people of color—the majority of the people. Although our constitution has inspired generations, even those that it leaves in the cold, it remains a dim ember of its true potential.

Now picture a constitutional convention not dominated by landowners, men, colonizers, or the independently wealthy. Instead, picture a cybernetic congress harnessing the aspirations of *all* people, hashed out collectively, rebooting the constitutional enterprise with an entirely new syntax. Imagine a convention where marginalized voices were not peripheral but at the heart of the discussion, informing a complex discourse on rights and responsibilities that mapped onto the contours of real lives.

Across a million screens such discourse would flicker, a neon haze of a convention that would draft a true people's constitution that was truly *for* us. A constitution for the whole of humanity, not cuffed by an archaic notion of borders. A constitution that not only keeps government out of our lives when we don't want it but also ensures its support for individuals and groups when we need it.

A feminist constitution.

Here is a starting place:

We the People, in Order to Defend Our Humanity . . .

Much has been made of the poetically expressed right to the "pursuit of happiness" in the Declaration of Independence. While it is in no way legally binding, it is an idea that still powerfully shapes our sense of the evanescent, intangible part of liberty and has played host to the projections of countless interested parties through the centuries. Whatever happiness means to you, it seems there's some musing about a right to have it in that epistolary founding document.

But that idea is terribly limiting. Happiness is not, as some might suggest, the ultimate goal of life. A good word to consider in lieu of "happiness" is the ancient Greek word *eudaimonia*. It is often mistranslated as "happiness," revealing how beholden we are to this diminished view of human flourishing in the modern age, but it is better understood as meaning "living a good life for a human being." It means to flourish in a fullness of practice, to dance through a full range of human experience—from the most pleasurable emotions, states, and practices to the thoroughly unpleasant ones. It means to live a life of meaning.

Eudaimonia excludes oppression: anything that restrains the full flight of your humanity, a flight on which you may make your own mistakes and endure your own pain. A *eudaimonic* constitution, then, would concern itself with providing for the preconditions of human flourishing. This is the approach a feminist constitution would take.

... Establish Justice, Ensure Freedom from Violence, And Freedom to Be

It would, of course, organize a government—and, for the purposes of our utopian dream, let us suppose that this "government" could take any form: collectivist or hierarchical—but it would place the rights and responsibilities of the people who made up the society at its very center.

Our constitution would begin with the negative liberties. While the current US Constitution outlines various freedoms "from" government intrusion, our constitution would also define freedom from other collective forces: corporations, majority religions, gender norms, prejudicial violence, wealth inequality, and so on. It would make provision for the fact that a child being bullied in school for her sexual orientation, or one forced to live under a highway overpass, could never feel free; it would acknowledge that freedom is not abstract but *lived*.

Our new constitution would recognize that liberty cannot only be conceived as negative freedoms from intrusion but also ought to be framed in terms of positive freedoms—the freedom "to be." That bullied child or homeless neighbor cannot be free without government support. While government can limit freedom, it is also necessary for its full realization. Here lie our guarantees of gainful employment, education, health care, security, and shelter. And this positive freedom branches off to a number of fascinating places.

For example, consider the freedom to create the community you want. Today, American law would understand this as a freedom from intrusion into your private life. But what if instead we saw it as freedom to build a family of any shape and size with society's *material support* behind you, including multigenerational households, queer houses, poly families, and more, all recognized as valid families worthy of any number of material accommodations provided by the government—special homes, financial remittances, childcare, freedom from policing kinship? The feminist constitution would ensure that no one would prohibit your community, and further, that the law and government would help you build it.

The Right of a Person to Have Sovereignty Over Their Body Shall Not Be Infringed . . .

While the right to *be* would surely encompass the right to bodily autonomy, the feminist constitution, unlike the US Constitution, would explicitly establish this guarantee as both a negative and positive liberty.

For too long, the notion of a constitutional right to privacy—a negative right from intrusion rather than a right *to* something—has been the precarious foundation for the jurisprudence of women's liberty. For example, it serves as the legal reasoning for a woman's right to an

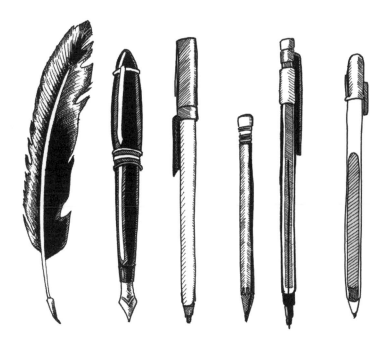

abortion. Supreme Court Justice William O. Douglas's famous argument was that a right to privacy existed in the "penumbras" and "emanations" of other constitutional rights; this legal innovation, so essential for so many, was nevertheless a sign of our constitution's fundamental inequality. In spite of its lofty symbolism, it remains chronically inadequate for the tasks of mass democracy.

A right to privacy divined in such a way—while providing a theoretical guarantee against government intrusion—also inoculates the government from any obligation to *ensure* that a person *can* access an abortion. If it is a private affair, it can neither be publicly funded nor publicly guaranteed.

A right to privacy is essential, but what is violated when a person is denied the right to an abortion is only thinly connected to privacy. She is being denied her *right to bodily autonomy* (not yet recognized in American law). The same is true of trans women denied public funding for health care, hormone therapy, and reassignment surgeries; or when someone is arrested for carrying condoms because they can be used as "evidence" by police to claim that person is a sex worker; or when women of color are arrested for "manifesting prostitution" simply for expressing their political views, by leaning in to talk to someone through a car window, or asking police officers to identify themselves, as Arizona state law currently permits.

But the common denominator here is a question of bodily autonomy, which disarticulates into these crucial concerns: what our bodies are for, how we may put them to use, and who ultimately gets to decide. At present, our abstractly thin rights to contraception and reproductive choice are guarded by a right that is, at best, orthogonal to it. A true constitution that guarded us all would spell out a right to bodily autonomy *unambiguously*. "My body, my choice" would be at the core of this constitution, not an afterthought that we struggle to pin to words written neither by nor for us.

. . . And Liberty of Both Kith and Self Shall Be Secure

These constitutional guarantees are further cemented by the idea that *groups*, as well as individuals, have rights. Currently, American courts treat individuals, not groups, as the carriers of rights, but this notion in practice often ends up annihilating meaningful individual freedom when it is under threat from informal collective forces like racism, sexism, or queerphobia. The health of communities would have to be seen as intimately related to the health and welfare of individuals: our constitution would see groups in society as rights holders. Such a perspective would obviate the individualization of terroristic crimes like rape, revealing them instead as human rights violations that constitute a crime against the body politic as well as an individual person.

This differs sharply from "corporate personhood," which allows a corporate entity's "rights" to trump that of the individual—by protecting individual rights *through* the prism of the group, not taking them away. But our utopian constitution understands that one cannot live freely if one exists in a collective under constant attack, say on account of gender, sexuality, or race—these are identities not bounded by strict spatial limits the way a corporation is.

This nimble vision allows for a fuller constitutional recognition of where meaningful rights lie and how they may be defended and made real. It codifies the idea that we must all stand together to guarantee *one another's* rights.

These Rights Shall Not Be Subject to the Vagaries of Markets or Depravation

An ideal constitution would take this seriously and begin from the premise of autonomy, woven into collective responsibility. In other words, we should not only avoid hindering each other's lives but also share in the responsibility for helping one another secure the conditions of a livable life, through guaranteed public funding for health, education, transport, housing, and energy on hitherto unimagined scales. Imagine if privatizing a school or a railway line was understood as a violation of peoples' rights; the right to access such things helps to secure other rights.

Not only would there be a right to reproductive health care *as such*, but also a shared understanding that this right can only be said to exist if any person, anywhere, is able to materially *access* that care—again, a freedom *to*, not just a freedom *from*. We could not allow cost or distance to be obstacles. To have a right to reproductive health care would mean, in a way clearly spelled out in constitutionally florid script, a right to feel it, touch it, and sense it, at no cost to you. It would be what we owe one another.

This would mean that reproductive health care would be publicly funded, up to and including all transport costs; contraception, being essential to such health, would also not be subject to one's ability to afford it.

This connection, between the immanent right one possesses and the guaranteed material means of *living* that right, would be the new constitutional framework whence all else would follow.

These rights would not be penumbras and emanations. They would be the bright suns unto themselves.

All Shall Have a Right to the Conditions Necessary For Life and to Dignity

The term "right to life" was long ago co-opted by the Far Right in their quest to invent personhood for fetuses even as it was denied to women. But what would a true right to life applied to us *all* look like?

A right to life for transgender people would mean a right to all the medical care and self-alteration necessary to fashion a livable life for ourselves, along the same lines of our hypothetical right to reproductive health care, and inaugurated for the same reasons. A right to life, period, would mean a right to a home, a right to food, a right to be free from prejudice and its manifold violent manifestations. It would mean fundamentally rethinking "criminal justice" and regarding the mission of any system worthy of that name as one that puts rehabilitation and community building at the center of its enterprises.

What results is a jurisprudence that is meaningfully intersectional, responds to the intricate questions of life and law with grace, and begins from the experiential reality of the lives of real people. The high-minded obscurity of constitutional law is a symptom of its origins, a vision of society that flies high at ten-thousand feet.

But a feminist constitution begins from the ground up: it asks what we need in order to live and flourish and then provides the sustenance for it, for it trusts us to know what we need to be free.

Katherine Cross *is a published sociologist and PhD student at the CUNY Graduate Center. She also serves on the board of the Sylvia Rivera Law Project and the Third Wave Fund in New York City.*

Ruth Tam *is a web producer at DC's NPR affiliate, WAMU. She has written and illustrated for the* Washington Post, PBS NewsHour, *and* Global Post. *She lives in Washington, DC, where she enjoys cheese, beer, and talking to strangers.*

Flag for the United Nations of Magical Girls

NICOLE KILLIAN

This flag represents the land which has been declared a utopia for the United Nations of Magical Girls. We come from near, we come from far, and we've come together to spread our power together.

Nicole Killian's work investigates how the structures of the internet, mobile messaging, and shared online platforms affect contemporary interaction and shape cultural identity. At the American Comparative Literature Association Annual Conference, she recently presented ongoing research, Sailor Moon ★ Glitter Text+Graphic Design ✓. Image by Studio Set.

The New Word Order

AMY JEAN PORTER

The following are examples of successful etymological reconditioning of words that had become trite and/or meaningless in the early twenty-first century.

Amy Jean Porter *is an artist. She has had solo exhibitions in New York, Chicago, Los Angeles, and Paris. Her work has been featured in publications such as* Cabinet, The Awl, Flaunt, jubilat, Meatpaper, *and* McSweeney's.

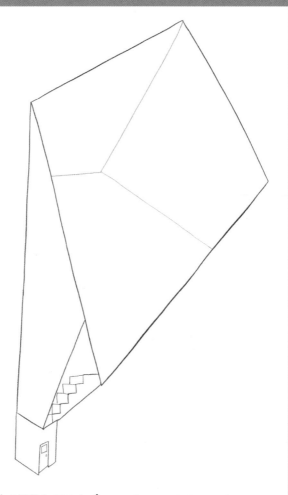

CRAFT /KRAFT/ NOUN 1) THE CORNERSTONE OF A
RESIDENTIAL POD. "THE CRAFT WAS MADE FROM THE
ORE OF AN ASTEROID" 2) AN ACTIVITY REQUIRING
GREAT SKILL "THE CRAFT OF HOUSE BLOOMING WAS
ESSENTIAL TO THE COMMUNITY"

PhDP

PRIN·CESS /'PRINSES/ NOUN 1) AN ADVANCED
DOCTORAL DEGREE. "AFTER DECADES OF EXTREME FOCUS
AND DEDICATION, HE FINALLY ACHIEVED HIS PRINCESS
DEGREE" 2) SOMEONE WHO IS UNABASHEDLY DRIVEN
"THE PRINCESS WORKED HARD AND MADE CREATIVE
LEAPS FAR BEYOND THE BOX"

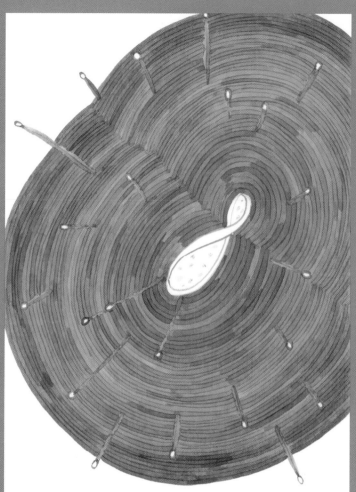

QUIRK·Y /'KWƏRKĒ/ NOUN 1) SUB^{2}ATOMIC PARTICLE THAT COMPRISES DARK MATTER. "PHYSICISTS BELIEVE THE ELUSIVE QUIRKY MAY LEAD THE WAY TO ALTERNATE UNIVERSES" 2) AN UNUSUAL TALENT OR UNEXPLAINED ABILITY "SHE HAD THE QUIRKY OF BEING ABLE TO SEE FIVE MINUTES INTO THE FUTURE"

SHRILL /SHril/ NOUN 1) INTERGALACTIC SPACE CREATURE THAT RESEMBLES A TERRESTRIAL SQUID "THE SHRILL SAT SILENT AND UNBLINKING AS IT KEPT WATCH OVER THE MILKY WAY"

WHIM·SY /ˈ(H)WIMZĒ/ NOUN **1)** A CLOUD FORMATION NOT CREATED BY LOCAL CLOUD-SEEDING OPERATIONS. "THE SMALL WHIMSY DRIFTED ACROSS THE SKY"
2) A THING THAT IS UNEXPECTED OR SURREAL "SHE WOKE UP SUDDENLY **AND** RECALLED **HER DREAM OF** CATS' WINGS AND OTHER **WHIMSIES"**

Justice

MARIAME KABA
ILLUSTRATION BY BIANCA DIAZ

The ocean is a special kind of blue-green and I'm standing on the shore watching a woman drown. My friends and family members are witnessing the same scene, or maybe it looks different to their eyes. They are grieving; I am not. I turn to my mother (who is a man) and whisper in his ear: "vengeance is not justice." And again "vengeance is not justice." I let the wind carry my words because human beings (even highly evolved ones) can't hear spirits.

I was sixteen when I died.

Darn, I did it again. I rushed to the end of the story before telling the beginning. I am one of those girls. You know what I mean; the kind of girl who eats dessert for dinner and reads the end of the book first. Everyone calls me impatient. Impatient should be my first name.

I love water and swimming. My father (who claims no gender) says that I must be descended from a fish and not a person. Mama says that he should have named me Aqua. Everyone seems to want to call me by a different name than my actual one, which is Adila though my friends call me Addie.

I live in Small Place (SP). If someone asked me to describe the sights, sounds, and smells of home, I'd say that SP is very green. I mean you can smell the green and the salt water and you can hear the wind rustling through the trees. We're family in SP. No, we aren't all related but we trust and love each other. While arguments and conflicts happen, we always resolve them. My parents are SP's chief peace-holders. If you are wondering how one becomes a chief peace-holder, it's simple really. Anyone over twenty years old is eligible. Every five years, a representative group of SP residents gather to consider candidates. Peace-holders are not special or better than anyone else in SP. The only requirements are a desire to serve and a commitment to embody and hold true to our community values. Those values are revisited, reviewed, and sometimes revised annually. Peace-holders' primary responsibilities are to make sure that all of our conflicts are swiftly and peacefully addressed.

Once, I asked Mama why he thought that he was selected as a chief peace-holder. He looked at me for a moment and then said: "I was over twenty years old, willing to serve, and I never forget our common humanity." Mama said that I am good at holding others and myself in our humanity. I'm not sure what he means. I do know that everyone makes mistakes and that we all deserve a chance to be held accountable for them so that we can do and be better next time. Maybe that's like my life philosophy or something. Anyway, what I love the most about living in SP is that we look out for one another; when one person in our community experiences harm, all of us are harmed. It's one of our most sacred and important values.

Though my parents are peace-holders, all of us are circle-keepers. We discuss all of our issues in circle. We celebrate in circle. We mourn in circle. Basically, circles are how we communicate and how we connect. Anyone in our community can call and keep a circle at any time and for any reason. There are no special skills to learn; all you need is to listen and to make space. All ages are included.

I mentioned that we're family in SP. We are a close-knit community but we often get visitors from other places. Last month, for example, a woman visited SP. She is a distant relative of our neighbors. She came from somewhere called Earth, which is very far indeed. There's nothing memorable about the Earth visitor (EV). Her hair is long and brown. She's pale like she doesn't spend a lot of time in the sun. The only thing that stood out is that she walked around SP carrying a knife in her purse. She said that it was in case she "ran into trouble." She added that on Earth, "women could never be too careful." I didn't understand what she meant. What kind of trouble would you need a knife for? And why would you be in more danger if you identified as a woman? If anything happened, she could just call a circle and together we'd address the issue.

We never locked our doors in SP and our Earth visitor (EV) insisted that this was unsafe. "What if someone wants to steal something from the house or what if they want to hurt someone?" she asked. My mother told her that everything in our house was community property and could be used by anyone. There is no such thing as private property in SP so no one had reason to steal from anyone else when they could simply share what others had. Besides, everyone in SP had their basic needs of food, clothing, and shelter met. Health care and education are also freely provided to all members of the community. EV then asked my father if they were afraid for me and my siblings' safety. My father simply shook their head and went to the kitchen to make dinner. Daddy is not the talkative one in our family.

I was so confused by EV's questions that I kept the dictionary tab on my computer open. I looked up words that I didn't understand like "fear" and "stealing." I read the definition of "fear" as "an unpleasant emotion caused by the belief that someone or something is dangerous, likely to cause pain, or a threat." This definition led me to look up more words like "dangerous" and "threat." While I was searching the web, I found a story called a *folktale* about how people on Earth address conflict and harm. Basically, it goes something like this:

While swimming across a pond, Sis Goose was caught by Brer Fox, who in some versions of the story is a sheriff. A sheriff is a police officer in case you don't know. I had to look that up too. We have no police in SP. Anyway, Sis gets pissed off because she believes that she has the right to swim in the pond. After all, she's not bothering anyone. She's just minding her own business. So Sis decides to sue Brer Fox. But when the case gets to court, Sis Goose looks around and sees that besides the sheriff who is a fox, the judge is a fox, the prosecuting and defense attorneys are ones too and even the jury is comprised entirely of foxes. Sis Goose doesn't like her chances. Sure enough, at the end of the trial, Sis Goose is convicted and immediately executed. The jury, judge, sheriff, and the attorneys all picked at her bones, which seems even crueler. The moral of the story is: "When all the folks in the courthouse are foxes and you are just a common goose there isn't going to be much justice for you."

I worried about this place called Earth and decided that it must be a terrible place to breed such scared, mistrustful, and cruel people. I was glad to be living in SP and resolved to keep my distance from Earth.

At dinner, EV resumed her relentless questioning. She asked where all of the criminals were housed. When we stared blankly, she became agitated and yelled "the bad people, the bad people, where do you put them?" My mother said that there was no such thing as bad people, only people who sometimes did a bad thing. Our visitor laughed bitterly. "Okay then," she said, "where do you put the people who do bad things?" Finally, I spoke up. "We don't put them anywhere because we all do bad things sometimes and through our relationships with each other we acknowledge the harm we've caused and then we do our best to try to repair it." EV looked at me like I had grown another head. "You have no prisons here, no jails?" "No," was our collective response. Then Mama asked: "How exactly do your prisons and jails address the needs of those who have experienced harm?" EV responded that jails and prisons offered accountability and punishment and that a strict justice system is especially important for women. My father asked if punishment was justice and added: "How do those who are locked in your prisons and jails heal? Are they improved by the experience?" That was their word limit for the day, I think.

Our ways and values were alien to EV and she was clearly disturbed by them. That night, I did some research about the punishment system on Earth and was shocked that the harmed person played almost no role in the process. The trials (I looked up that word too) were the State of Indiana v. the name of the person who caused harm. Also, it didn't seem like all of the "crimes" were necessarily very harmful or that all of the harms were considered "crimes." I read one story of a young girl who was raped and they actually blamed her for drinking too much at a party. The person responsible for her pain didn't have to acknowledge the harm they caused or make amends. In SP, the entire community would have focused first on the needs of the young girl, then we would use circles to discuss what had happened and insist that the person who committed the harm take responsibility. They would be assigned several members of the community to support and guide them in completing the agreed-on restitution. I have to admit though that I had a hard time imagining such a thing as rape happening in our community.

One day after school, I went for a swim. I got naked and dived in the ocean. I was floating with my eyes closed while thinking about my friend Noliwe, which brought a smile to my face. Noliwe is my most favorite person in SP next to my parents and siblings. I was jolted out of my daydream when I heard someone approach. I opened my eyes and saw that EV was staring at me. She had a knife in her hand.

I was sixteen when I died.

I was killed by a visitor from a place called Earth who couldn't believe that there were no prisons in SP. Mine was the second murder ever in our community and it fell to my parents as chief peace-holders to ensure that the harm caused was addressed. For days, people across our community convened, communed, celebrated, and consoled each other in circle. There were talking circles, mourning circles, circles of support, and celebration circles. They happened at dawn, in midmorning, in the evening, and in the dead of night. For days, members of

SP told stories about my life through tears, anger, and laughter. There was, however, no talk of punishment or vengeance. Neither would bring me back.

After weeks of centering my family members and friends and of showering them with love, support, and food, the SP community turned its attention to my killer. EV was included in all of the previous circles and so she had experienced the community's outpouring of grief and loss. She heard stories about my life. She knew the extent of the pain felt by my community. After she killed me, she turned herself in to my parents. Her first words to them were: "Where will you put me?" They responded in unison: "In circle." And so it was that EV came to understand the impact of her actions on an entire community. And so it was that she experienced remorse for her actions and sought to make amends. And so it was that my community held EV in her humanity while seeking to hold her accountable for her actions.

The first murder that occurred in SP happened decades earlier. The ancestors created our Justice Ritual in response. After several days of mourning and celebrating the life of the person killed, the killer's life and actions are explored. In a series of circles, participants discuss why the violence happened, how it happened, and who was harmed. Community members are asked to stand in the shoes of the person who committed the harm, to consider the conditions that underlie their actions, and to examine their own roles in perpetuating those conditions. It was an acknowledgement that no matter how hard we try to purge ourselves of emotions like jealousy, envy, and anger, they remain within us and can negatively impact our relationships. Remaining aware of this is important to maintaining peace.

When circles have been exhausted, the killer is taken to the ocean, tied up, and dropped into the water. This empathy ceremony takes place in front of the entire community. The immediate family members of the victim are given the option of saving the life of the killer or letting them drown. If the family saves the person's life, they are then required to take the place of the person killed within the community. They are expected to pay a debt for the life taken for however long the harmed parties deem necessary but they do so within the community, living as integrated members.

I saw my father motion to my mother. He nodded his head. EV was rescued from the ocean. When we hold each other in our humanity, what other outcome could there be? Vengeance is not justice.

I was sixteen when I died and my name was Adila, which means "justice."

Mariame Kaba *is an organizer, educator, and writer living in Chicago. Her work focuses on ending violence, dismantling the prison industrial complex, transformative justice, and supporting youth leadership development. She is the founder and director of Project NIA, a grassroots organization with a vision to end youth incarceration.*

Bianca Diaz *is a Mexican American artist and educator living and working in Chicago. Using art and education as her tools, she strives to be instrumental in the collaborative creation of these communities.*

Interview with Lauren Chief Elk

The following is excerpted from an interview an editor conducted over the phone with antiviolence organizer and victims' service provider Lauren Chief Elk on October 10, 2014. Chief Elk is the cofounder of Save Wiyabi Project, and she writes and organizes to develop community-based responses to gender-based violence that reject policing and the criminal justice system. The first time one of us talked to her in person she told us that a meeting like ours—two people coming together to support one another—is justice.

It's hard to talk about responses to gender-based violence in a utopian way because obviously you hope that in a feminist utopia there would be no gender-based violence. But assuming in this great, wonderful world we're dreaming of, there would still be interpersonal conflict and people would still sometimes hurt each other—how would you like to see individuals and communities?

That's a good way to start this conversation. Because, right, duh, in a feminist utopia, gender-based violence is obviously not there. Solved.

[*Laughs*] End of interview.

The book *The Revolution Starts at Home* proposes a world where we all have the skills to help each other so we're not relying on anonymous hotlines. That idea is how I've come to conceptualize the organizing and work that I do. My goal as an organizer and service provider is that I want to end violence, yes, but I also want to get people to feel comfortable supporting each other and having difficult conversations. I want to help people become comfortable with being uncomfortable, and incorporating this into work outside of hotlines and victim service agencies is a big goal.

One of the themes we keep returning to in working on this project is that a feminist utopia would require continued work: even if you eradicate gender-based violence, we'd have to be vigilant to keep it that way. What are the ways that you think communities could hold each other accountable to do that? I'm not talking about bystander intervention in the sense of a big protective guy standing between a drunk girl and a predator at a party, but in a larger sense of collective responsibility.

In the framework of prison abolition and dismantling the carceral state and moving toward transformative justice interventions, we have to let go of the idea that if something goes bad you call the police. We have to reimagine safety. I think people hold on to the police because it gives such a strong yet false sense of safety. We must uproot and examine the mainstream ideas of safety. And the same with justice. The prison system lives inside of us. We think justice is about locking up the bad guys. In reality, that's not what's happening now. People ask me constantly, "Well, Lauren, if we don't have prisons what are we going to do with the child molesters and rapists?" And my response to that is, "The same thing we're doing now because those aren't the people in prison." We don't treat victims with decency and respect, or afford them any type of care. Supporting people, is the alternative to what we have now.

Let's say that, in the feminist utopia, someone has experienced harm at the hands of another community member, either inadvertently or purposefully, and now needs support. What do they do?

We still need institutional mechanisms for crisis response. We still need systems of accountability, so that someone who has been harmed knows who to turn to and who can arbitrate justice. We will always need structure and rules; but it needs to be a good structure. I talk to my grandma, and she tells me what was set up traditionally in our communities. There were elders who led and there was a structure to address matters of hurting each other. The first step was believing the person and asking them what they want and how they want their aggressor to be held accountable. What is this going to mean for your personal healing? There's no blanket way where it's predetermined how we handle a situation. It's victim-centric justice.

We use the word "community" to mean many, many different things. Often when people talk about addressing harms, people are talking about the state as the unit of redress. What communities do you see stepping up to fill this role?

When we talk about community justice or community organizing, it can't be a romanticized version of community. Today, people leave their communities because something happens and their people aren't helping them: their community turns and punishes them instead of the person doing the harm. People abandon community because of that.

We are in a time of using movements to find a community of people invested in doing feminist antiviolence work. New groups are forming. When we talk about "community" it can mean a whole number of things. Where do you go out? Who do you feel safe with? It might be where you're actually living, your workspace, your family, your extended family—whatever. That term can be really expandable and elastic. It doesn't just have to mean where you live, your neighbors, and your county. It's the people with whom you are operating.

We've been speaking mostly about helping people who have been victimized, but do you have a thought on how, in the utopia, we would approach people who do something wrong?

I think this is probably the most difficult part—taking this seriously. There's going to be someone who is best friends or brothers or boyfriends with the person who does the harm, and their immediate response is going to be to protect. I think this is where we get into the different forms of accountability. Let's not only ask the [victimized] person what they want, but also provide options. What will justice be and how will we *all* contribute to it? Part of the practice is having lots of open dialogue—and asking why we want so badly to protect abusers. One of our favorite hobbies is feeling bad for rapists. [*Laughs*] "Oh he's such a good guy. He's such a good athlete. He does such good work. We can't just say they're bad people because they murdered their girlfriend."

It sounds like in your vision rejecting the carceral state doesn't mean rejecting punishment. It just means figuring out who is in control of this punishment and what is its purpose.

Yes. There needs to be a structure, just not a violent structure that creates more trauma and victims instead of justice.

Those options would then include, what, expulsion from the community? I think this is the hardest thing. Are there other forms of sanctions that you think combat violence rather than perpetuate it?

After working so much with really awesome lawyers and learning more about the civil process, I think financial retribution is my favorite form of accountability right now.

Me too!

When harms cost money on top of just the pain of harm itself—whether the person needed to drop out of school and seek medical care or quit their job—making someone financially accountable to you is really transformative.

I really despise the conversation around the civil process, when victims sue their rapists. There was this article from some liberal lefty group saying "Oh, we don't know about this whole financial retribution thing: Is there a price that will ever be justice?" But that's not for anyone to decide but the victims. They know what they need.

Not on My Block
Envisioning a World without Street Harassment

HANNAH GIORGIS

Being . . . a woman is an awful tragedy. Yes, my consuming desire to mingle with road crews, sailors and soldiers, bar room regulars—to be a part of a scene, anonymous, listening, recording—all is spoiled by the fact that I am a girl, a female always in danger of assault and battery. My consuming interest in men and their lives is often misconstrued as a desire to seduce them, or as an invitation to intimacy. Yet, God, I want to talk to everybody I can as deeply as I can. I want to be able to sleep in an open field, to travel west, to walk freely at night.

—Sylvia Plath

In my feminist utopia, I am human and my name is not "baby."

In my feminist utopia, I can walk down the street in peace. The sun shines, children play in a bursting hydrant, and my heart beats in tandem with their smiles. We are part of the same ecosystem, bodies floating through the city as though propelled by the warmth between us.

I pause to bask in the magic of the block and walk closer to the children, careful not to let the concrete geyser pull me, unsuspecting, into their aquatic games. We exchange smiles again—a moment that lingers in the thick summer air. When my neighbor walks out of his building into the same heavy air that cloaks the children and me, my smile doesn't fade.

I meet his gaze and nod, unafraid of the consequences. I *see* him and know he, too, exists in the same warm ecosystem. I invite him to share in the moment, refreshing us all. He accepts and joins us, pausing on his stoop to appreciate the universe for bringing us all together. After a moment, I start walking toward the train, passing children and neighbors with long, confident strides.

In my feminist utopia, the story can end here. I am able to interact with other members of my community and appreciate the splendor of a kaleidoscopic city without fear of violence. I can smile at a man and know that he feels the joy radiating from my body without the need to touch it. We can share the world's oldest hello without ever exchanging words.

Or, I can talk to my neighbor (or choose not to) without the exhausting calculus of violence prevention weighing heavily on my spirit and my tongue. I can pause my day to ask him or any man what moves him, what thought enters his mind as he first wakes up each morning, what it is he loves about himself and the world around him. When our conversation ends, I need not fear that he will take my interest in his complex humanity as an invitation for aggression. He will respect my boundaries and the situation need not escalate if I turn away before offering myself to him. If I express disinterest, that response will be honored and not prodded to the point of my exhaustion.

I am able to walk outside the place I call home at any time of day, in any outfit, and I do not have to invent a male partner to defend against street harassers. I do not have to debate the sometimes impossible financial burden of taking a cab home against the risk of encountering a man who will mistake my womanhood for an invitation to violence; I do not have to choose whether to be safe and broke or risk my safety and save my already-overburdened wallet.

In my feminist utopia, I am not just a set of legs crossing the street; I am more than a potential conquest. I can respond affirmatively to attention that respects the full range of my humanity; I can walk away if I am tired or rushing or simply not here for it. I am a person with a complex set of emotions, motivations, and experiences—and that is understood.

Hannah Giorgis *is a black feminist writer, organizer, and educator. She loves blogging at ethiopienne.com, having long conversations about envisioning a more liberated world, cooking Ethiopian food, and looking at Idris Elba.*

Raising Generation E (For Empathy)
The Final Frontier of Feminism

MINDI ROSE ENGLART

One day, not long ago, women said: enough.

Enough with focusing on half the population. They went beyond teaching their daughters self-esteem and self-defense. It became apparent that no matter how much they empowered girls, the next step was to finally and meaningfully address the underlying issues that caused their abuse—to really deal with the ways that gender inequality had made violence and greed toward women permissible and frequent.

Enough with traditional "family values" that reinforced obsolete gender norms. It was time to make entirely new values. Parents in this utopia modeled and rewarded empathy over defensiveness, reason over reaction, and conscience over compulsion. When young utopian children showed signs of violent sexuality, parents talked to them, without taboo and without shame, about their feelings and about ways to channel their frustration, sadness, or anger into something constructive and productive—to help rather than harm. To construct rather than destroy.

"Let's brainstorm," mothers and fathers said to their boys again and again across the utopian world. They said, "Not every feeling of aggression has to result in explosions; not every erection has to result in an orgasm. Not every feeling of powerlessness needs to result in an act of domination."

"Feelings pass," they said. "Feelings are messages. The ability to choose a response rather than react, to create rather than destroy, is what makes humans human."

And, of course, talking about feminism became easier because as young people explored gender as a spectrum, traditional cultural roles loosened. "Masculinity" was broadened to include sensitivity—both personal and political. The idea that some people are preyed on purely because of the body they were born into began to seem less like a fact of life and more like something that was messed up, unfair, and that needed to be changed.

But the surprising thing that really catalyzed change, made the last wave of feminism the final wave, was actually the radical changes to the legal system.

The traditional patriarchal way of punishing rather than treating just stopped working, because once the equal rights laws began to be enforced in earnest, the courts quickly overfilled, and the judges couldn't handle the caseloads. Eventually, it was impossible to prosecute and punish all the many people who had harmed women and children. The legal system fell open and fell apart. With so many cases, the law became too complex for even those in the system that enforced it to understand and enact. Once people realized that the law was one thing, but real justice began with empathy, the rule of law began to morph organically into the rule of reparation.

That's when the world looked to lessons from the past and began to meaningfully institute the Law of Restorative Justice. Nowadays, judges and juries are convened only for the most heinous cases. But the majority of bad acts are dealt with by the community tribunals—teams of supporters who hold space for acts of restitution to happen, one person at a time. A victim of any rare act of violence—including remnants of the past, like rape—now files a report, and a tribunal is convened. Mediators provided by the community and selected for their emotional intelligence facilitate this process. Surrounded by supporters, the victim has the chance to speak about the damage that has been done and declares the actions they need as reparation, to make them whole again. Life can begin to move forward for everyone.

Empathetic people in helping professions became leaders, both inside and outside the law. Professions like social work, nursing, and education—once typically held by women who just scraped by—are now well-paid and prestigious. The ability to support others is today's most marketable skill. Celebrities are no longer football stars or fashion models. They're the people who make the biggest differences to other people.

Take a look at the history books. The newest ones detail the last wave of feminism's fight and ultimate victory: full equality. You'll see that some states tried to secede, that even some women tried to keep things the same. New cultures don't arise overnight; change takes time.

Now, the young people of Generation E fear car accidents, natural disasters, and megalomaniacs. But they don't fear violence. Everyone can walk down the street gazing up at the night sky, not looking behind them in fear, because people of all genders are busy—actualizing themselves and each other. These active, caring young people have more time, money, and energy for creativity, love, and support than their parents could have even imagined. Evolution is a funny thing. You can't rush it, but you can't hold it back.

Mindi Rose Englart *is a single mom of a lovely daughter she had at age forty. Mindi is an artist, an author, and a creative writing teacher at an arts magnet high school in New Haven, Connecticut. She is the founding editor of* Etcetera *literary magazine, a 2010 Surdna Grant recipient, the author of twelve books for children, and a contributing writer to* The Lucretia Society, *a play that addresses sexual violence against women.*

If Absence Was the Source of Silence

REGINALD DWAYNE BETTS

Some things my sons would never hear,
not because of my reluctance to speak,
or the thief that has silenced his mother's
tongue, his grandmother's tongue,
turned the stare of the woman who sees me
turn a corner with Newport in hand,
far too early for the sun to be out,
the sky and ground as dark as the fear
& history she swallows as she crosses
into what might as well be ongoing traffic.
Those bedrooms where trust became carnage
will be all mirage, all the invention
of those uncomfortable with this world.
What I mean is that we lack a map
for the place we plead every name of God
we know to show us. With that map

my sons' awakening would be so unlike my own,
where helplessness and rage drown us.
No long conversations about what the hands
of men might do. His hands, my own.
I keep trying to turn what I have to say
into sense: When I was twelve and a friend
told me of men offering her money for sex
and she no older than me, arms not strong
enough to carry her own weight, let alone
push her past all the men who wanted
to own what is hers. & this was only the first
of a story that would keep coming back.
The numbered hurt. Rape, its aftermath
& this account of trauma, my boys
would never know if the world were different.
If war did not mean how many soldiers
have imagined the body of a woman
just more land to be plundered. I keep
trying to turn this into sense. My sons
will hear from me a story about how hands
like theirs, like mine, have made something
wretched of the memories of women
we love. This is true. & there is a map
to take us to all that hurt. Some silence
saying it all. But let's say the world is ours.
Let's add that to the accounting. On that day
all the silenced tongues would have
no memory of cars that became dungeons,

of friends who became the darkness
that swallows all until only rage & hurt
remains. No memory because absence
would be the source of silence, all
the things that happen now, as if
a part of being, would not be—
and my sons' lives would be carved
out of days in which their hands
& bodies do not suggest weapons,
days where all their mothers
& sisters can walk down any street
in America with the freedom
that comes from knowing
you will be safe, after dusk or during
those moments just before dawn.
A time when what I give them is not
this world circled by harms that even
here, I have named all too inadequately.

Reginald Dwayne Betts *is the author of* Bastards of the
Reagan Era, A Question of Freedom, *and the collection of
poems* Shahid Reads His Own Palm.

What Would a Feminist Utopia Look Like for Parents of Color?

VICTORIA LAW

Let's close our eyes and imagine what that might look like: a world where all children are welcome and communities take a collective responsibility for raising the young people in their midst.

It is the afternoon and you are in a bookstore. You encounter a display of children's books featuring small heroes of a variety of genders and faces. There are picture books with adventures about Chinese girls climbing forbiddingly high mountains to reach dragons, Mexican girls transforming into superheroes, Black children flying through the night sky, white bunnies trying to transform themselves into Black girls. There are more books about everyday adventures of childhood, a Black boy on a snowy day in the city or a Korean boy searching for a bagel in his small village.

For a fleeting instant, you remember your own childhood experiences with books in which nearly every character in every book was white. Books featuring children of color were only pulled out during certain months. But then your mind comes back to the display before you and, faced with so many wonderful choices, you let that memory fade away.

Around the corner, there are rows and rows of dolls—a toy for a child of any gender to learn to love and care for. The selection isn't limited to white baby dolls with pale skin and blue eyes. You can choose dolls that are clearly Black, Asian, Latino, Native American, or white. You can choose from a variety of dolls that are mixed race. You can choose a doll that is clearly a boy, a doll that is clearly a girl, or a doll that is not clearly either gender. You can choose a doll that reflects the skin color, the shape, size, gender, and ethnicity of the baby you are shopping for. Or you can choose one that is totally different. But the choices are endless and no single skin tone or body size dominates the shelves.

"Sure is different from when I was growing up," you murmur as you reach out to feel whether one doll's curly black hair feels silky or stiff, and then get in line for the register to bring her home.

As you head home, with your doll and way more books than you had anticipated buying, you pass a group of neighborhood children running around and yelling. "No, it's *my* turn to be John Brown! " a girl, probably no older than four or five, shouts, stomping her feet. "You aw-reddy got to be John Brown!"

You see Ms. Agnes sitting nearby. Even though Ms. Agnes has chosen not to have children of her own, she's taken on the responsibility of watching the children on the block this afternoon. It's not surprising—most people on the block take turns watching the children so that they can safely play outside. Act X102Y now allows parenting and caregiving to be considered paid work and many have taken the opportunity to raise their children full time, but the rotation allows parents and other caregivers time to work on personal projects or simply sit in peace for a short time. It also means that the community watches over the children, including breaking up arguments and settling disputes, instead of turning that responsibility over to total strangers.

You greet Ms. Agnes and ask about their game.

"Oh, them?" Ms. Agnes looks up from her crossword puzzle. "They're playing John Brown. MeiMei has been clamoring to be John Brown for the past half hour." She goes on to explain that Jane's mothers had taken her and several other children to a history exhibit that included John Brown last weekend. Excited about John Brown's liberation attempts, the children spread the word about his heroics to their friends. Now, their new favorite game is "John Brown," one in which they all take turns holding up the train and getting guns to arm the slaves—regardless of their own skin color or gender identity. They also seemed undeterred that the historical John Brown was unsuccessful (or that he was ultimately hanged).

For a moment, you feel a fleeting pang of envy. You

didn't know about John Brown until you were past college: stories of resistance and racial justice didn't make it into your history books. But before you have enough time to start feeling angry, Ms. Agnes asks, "You going to Jackie and Enrique's birthday party next weekend? It's over at the Punk House."

Unlike the other houses and apartments in the neighborhood that are either single people or families, the Punk House is a communal living situation of punks and artists in their early twenties who, like Ms. Agnes, are always ready to support neighborhood parenting. Kids love the Punk House. When the group first moved to town, they set up a basketball hoop and invited all the neighborhood children to use it anytime they wanted.

Local parents appreciate knowing neighbors will take a shift looking after their kids, but the punks really endeared themselves to their adult neighbors when they took in Cynthia and her babies after toxic mold was found in her apartment. One morning, seeing black mold spreading from behind her kitchen cabinets, Cynthia called a housing inspector. The inspector told her that it was extremely dangerous to small children, throwing Cynthia into a panic. Word spread and Enrique, one of the punks, offered Cynthia and her children his room while the landlord had the mold abated. Enrique spent those next two months sleeping on the couch and being woken in the morning by Cynthia's two-year-old, Zilla, jumping on him. The other members of the house developed friendships with the kids as well, teaching them to play their guitars and reading them stories.

"Maybe," you tell Ms. Agnes. At the last party, a toddler rode a tricycle into your shins. Punks seem to have very different ideas about indoor and outdoor activity. Still, bruised shins aside, their parties are always fun.

"Hey, Ms. Agnes! Hey, Xiaolong." Dylan skips down the street wearing sparkly purple high-tops and a matching cap that doesn't quite cover the riot of black curls. Jay-Jay wears all black and, against her pale skin and newly bleached hair, is in stark contrast. She moves more slowly than the fifteen-year-old.

"Hey, Dylan. Where you off to?" Ms. Agnes greets the glittering teen.

"Jay-Jay and I are going to the movies. Then we're gonna eat vegetarian sushi downtown," Dylan replies. As Dylan gestures, you notice that each fingernail sports a different color—all sparkle in the midafternoon sun.

"Oh! I forgot my purse!" Dylan exclaims. "Be right back!"

As Dylan races home, Jay-Jay turns to you and Ms. Agnes. "Dylan's growing up into a wonderful adult," Jay-Jay says quietly. "But those teen years are rough, so I'm trying to make sure that ze knows there are adults ze can talk to. I can only imagine how hard it is when you don't identify as a common gender that other kids are used to, as a 'boy' or 'girl.' But hopefully knowing that ze has people other than parents to go to will make it a little less difficult for Dylan." She pauses. "I never wanted to ask my parents anything about sex or relationships. Hopefully, Dylan will feel comfortable talking to me if ze ever has any questions. But for now, we're just going to giggle ourselves silly at the movies and then stuff ourselves with sushi."

Dylan comes flying down the block with a purse (sparkly purple of course) trailing behind like the tail of a kite. "I'm ready! Let's go, let's go, let's go before we miss the movie!"

You have to smile. At the same time, Jay-Jay's words make you feel a little wistful. Your mama didn't have that kind of support when you were growing up. Back then, it was assumed that every parent was responsible for his or her own children and should not expect others to help out. Even when your mama was involved in racial justice organizing, she was often expected to either leave you and your sister at home with a babysitter or, if she brought you along, to keep you quiet and well behaved. When you started school, she had to balance participating in planning meetings and discussions with quietly helping with homework on the sidelines.

And this all came at the end of the day, after she had worked eight to ten hours in an office to pay the bills. You were all tired and hungry, but your mama wanted a world in which you were all safe and taken care of. You're too young to remember them, but mama has told you that, when you were little, headlines often screamed about young children being shot to death by the police simply for walking down the street or for being Black. So, even if it meant that as a child you got dragged to meetings, ate takeout, and got to bed way too late several times a week, she was going to fight to make sure that you never had to worry about any of your children being targeted because of the color of their skin. Your mama didn't live long enough to see that vision come true, but you're getting to see some of the fruits of those struggles.

As you say goodbye to Ms. Agnes, you look over at the group of children still playing John Brown (the four-year-old has gotten her turn and now another child, one with dark brown skin and a pink bandana over part of his face, is the legendary abolitionist). You see other neighbors on the block—some gardening or reading or chatting while at the same time offering other sets of eyes to make sure that everyone, young and old, is safe. That everyone is truly seen. And you know that this is true for every other block in the city.

The weight of all the books in your bag reminds you that it's time to get going. It also makes you wonder how different your childhood would have been—how different your relationship would have been if instead of dedicating her free time to organizing and protesting, your mama could have spent her evenings reading books aloud to you. Suddenly, you can't wait to get home to your little one, curl up on the couch, and explore all the different people and worlds that these new books open up.

Victoria Law *is a writer, photographer, and mother. She is the author of* Resistance Behind Bars: The Struggles of Incarcerated Women *and the coeditor of* Don't Leave Your Friends Behind: Concrete Ways to Support Families in Social Justice Movements and Communities.

I Don't

SAM HUBER

Wedding, wedding, wedding, wedding,
You know a wedding ain't the thing.
                    —Nina Simone, "22nd Century"

When we were both miserable and single in the dystopia
that is college, my best friend T (a straight woman)
and I (a queer, ambivalently male-identified person)
hatched a plan to live together with our respective partners and raise children among the four or five or six of
us. The world was big and punishing, and we could not
imagine navigating it without each other's help. It was a
dream, a joke, framed for others as a desperate backup
and laughed about in deference to its legal and cultural
implausibility, but it got me through. Being happily partnered—to another T in another city; let's call him T2—
has not made that future any less appealing to me, and T1
and I have since taken some natural-enough baby steps

in its direction. In a new city, our postgrad apartments are a mere half block apart; a warm and noisy stream of undefined relations flows steadily between them. One of our favorite neighborhood bars is called Friends and Lovers. Still, the dream remains rather dreamy. What is the measure of that half block between our pretty good now and that improbable then?

An older memory, or class of memory, and more serious: As a child, I was always curious about those acquaintances of my parents' who were not Married with Children. How to place them? Could they really be *adults*, when adulthood meant spouses, strollers, mortgages, sedans, pets? If so, could they really be *partners* to each other from separate cities, with separate names and homes and bank accounts? Approaching adulthood, I've begun to wonder how conscious they were of being curiosities. I wonder if that awareness was a source of pain—when it wasn't, conceivably, a contrary kind of pleasure—great enough to lead some among them ultimately to wed, to bear children.

T1 and I and our stream of relations are all inventing our own ways of claiming adulthood, of populating our new lives, though they would never have occurred to my curious and ill-equipped younger self. I, with my boyfriend in another city, and T1, with her Friends and Lovers, are making our arrangement work, and I am proud of that and of us. But what to call it? Younger selves, distant relations, more conventional friends, insatiably curious government: How to convince you that yes, we are fine, these lives we are building together might just nurture all of the love we need in all of the ways we need it? And is it your business? Might we instead ask our government, our distant relations, even our younger selves to trust us more, to regard us a little less curiously?

Another memory, which is also a warning: On the morning that the Defense of Marriage Act was partially overturned, and then again two years later when the Supreme Court ruled same-sex marriage bans unconstitutional, my Facebook friends celebrated as if gay utopia had arrived. In 1963, James Baldwin wrote, "The vision people hold of the world to come is but a reflection, with predictable wishful distortions, of the world in which they live." In 2013, the same court to which the best-funded representatives of our movement successfully petitioned for DOMA's invalidation had gutted the Voting Rights Act just days before. Can such an institution ever be trusted to deliver our best future?

There are so many ways that one might build a life; so few of them fit in the marriage equality movement. Most same-sex marriage advocates disavow the regulatory implications of their campaign, though queer people, feminists, single parents, sex workers, anti-racist activists, and other sexually oppressed communities have fought for decades to make marriage visible as an instrument of legal oversight rather than a natural expression of monogamous love. Beneath its romantic veneer, marriage is a legal contract conferring a host of material benefits that remain inaccessible to the unmarried. Its privileged status is secured through these practical advantages and the simultaneous devaluation of all other chosen families, as Justice Anthony Kennedy made clear in his widely circulated majority decision legalizing same-sex marriage nationally in June 2015. He wrote: "No union is more profound than marriage, for it embodies the highest ideals of love, fidelity, devotion, sacrifice, and family." The more liberal contingent of the marriage equality camp claims to have no issue with dissident sexual practices that fall outside their program, instead insisting that they are fighting simply for the right to marry, and that marriage is but one common and meaningful option among many for structuring a partnership. But to do so is to deny the power—to exclude, to be celebrated, to claim all the state owes you—that makes marriage so appealing in the first place.

Alternate kinship structures cannot achieve sufficient state support until marriage gives up or shares its most defining features, beginning with the vast array of rights and entitlements that have been bundled exclusively to marriage at the expense of those individuals and families who cannot or will not enter into it. These include but are by no means limited to exclusive tax breaks, public assistance, shared health care, joint legal and financial status, medical decision-making and inheritance privileges, confidentiality of marital communications, child support rights, and expedited pathways to citizenship—all of which are denied to the unmarried.

Then there is the slew of extralegal but perhaps more visible perks: unique qualification for professional benefits, respect from acquaintances and strangers alike, a sheen of self-sufficiency resulting from privatized family support, an exclusionary sense of success defined negatively against the unmarried, religious approval in what remains a Christian-supremacist nation, and countless diffuse affirmations at every level of culture. All of which proceeds directly, of course, from the institution's historical baggage: dowries, arranged marriages, binary gender roles, the Moynihan Report, eugenics, antimiscegenation laws, et cetera, ad nauseam.

In the summer of 2015, the Supreme Court legalized same-sex marriage nationally, and there may be a case to be made for letting this expanded access stand rather than changing course by demanding marriage's abolition. Perhaps now that marriage equality has been won, its unprecedented activist and philanthropic infrastructure might be leveraged toward expanding services for people who won't or can't marry.

Either approach, though, if it is to be acceptable and sufficient, must land us in the same utopia: one where anything called "marriage" wouldn't look like a marriage at all. Once the institution has been stripped of its unique legal and economic incentives, the only reason for retaining the classification—for continuing to call your long-term monogamous partnership a marriage— would be a lingering attachment to its romantic prestige, which only confirms its inherent exclusions.

I dream of a future after marriage. So what is to replace it? Over the last couple of decades, promising templates have already begun to emerge. The 2006 statement "Beyond Same-Sex Marriage," signed by dozens of LGBTQ activists, scholars, and allies, lists "domestic partnerships, second parent adoptions, reciprocal beneficiary arrangements, joint tenancy and home-ownership contracts, health-care proxies, [and] powers of attorney" as examples of existing legal possibilities for nonnormative families in this country. In France, civil solidarity pacts (PACS) guarantee certain rights and benefits that more directly pertain to shared living arrangements than to romantic relationships, and they have become a popular alternative to marriage among heterosexual as well as same-sex couples.

These nascent alternatives offer glimpses of our utopia, but articulating a future from our current moment—on any scale, personal or global—feels a bit like shuffling a deck of cards: exciting and fruitful combinations may emerge, but they can only consist of the fifty-two options we start with. Ace, seven, two, queen. Marriage, polyamory, coparenting, friendship. A real utopia will require trading this deck for a new one, or stuffing the pack to bursting with more cards than it can fit. I don't pretend to have the fifty-third card. But let's shuffle the deck a bit anyway.

Most immediately, our government must disentangle the bundle of rights and privileges currently reserved for marriage so that we can mix and match benefits to best suit the particularities of our kinship networks. No one should be bullied by the state into contractual monogamy for fear of lost assets, lost citizenship status, or lost control in the event of an emergency.

Perhaps the most obvious consequence of divorcing marriage's privileges from romantic coupledom will be that many more of our friends stay single for longer, childless forever and mostly by choice. These will be incidental rather than defining details. Some of these single friends may live in our homes with us and our children, and those who don't will gladly accept our dinner invitations, because they will be less likely to drown in a sea of parental story-swapping among a unanimously and emphatically partnered friend group.

Building networks that do not abandon these single and childless friends will require not just the eradication of stigma, but the active expansion of social safety nets to include people without dependents; responsibility for illness and end-of-life care will shift from families to the state. Such reliance on plentiful and easily obtained public assistance will be routine for single as well as partnered individuals, because we will have learned from contemporary disability activists that mutual care can and should be bedrock. As Robert McRuer demands: "Not self-sufficiency but self-determination, not independence but interdependence."

More about those children, if we have any. The four or five or six of us who share the work of raising them will not need to worry about who's authorized to cosign their first leases—will land still be privately owned in our utopia?—or chaperone field trips. Our children will have friends raised in an unimaginable range of households, some of which might resemble our own. This diversity of family arrangements will not be fodder for teasing by our children's teachers or peers. At school, the books they read will be freed from the requisite, worn-out courtship narratives. Because sexist expectations of women's dependency and singles' stigma will have been dismantled along with marriage, a story about a female hero will chronicle her heroism without the parallel drama of shrewish resistance and ultimate submission to a male partner, competitor, or assailant.

Our children will have been brought to school by whichever parent was free that morning, which will rarely be an issue because few of us will work more than four hours a day. When domestic work is valued *as* work rather than as a gendered skill set—women's work, wives' work—or a full-time alternative to "real" employment, employers will have to allow for the fact that employees of all genders and relationship statuses have domestic, social, and emotional lives that demand much more of their attention than they are presently afforded.

The repercussions of this more permeable public-private barrier seem limitless, cascading: Parents will nurse in public; we will discuss sexuality and health openly and without shame; we will better acknowledge the sexual lives of young people and help them navigate their new desires in nonstigmatizing ways.

Because the family will have been deemphasized as the single sacred social unit, and because shared blood will have been deemphasized as the single sacred criterion for family membership, it will no longer make sense to bequeath wealth from parents to children. Inheritance perpetuates and expands the gap between rich and poor, but the nuclear family will no longer be discrete and coherent enough to bear this function, and the expansion of state services will have obviated any interest in wealth accumulation, anyway. And taxes. Taxes! In someone else's utopia they will have figured out a better way to share collective responsibility for welfare and public services. In the meantime, the eradication of marriage will mean the eradication of tax cuts for the married.

Culturally, relational forms will lose their coding as signs of individual success or failure, leaving us freer to define those poles on our own terms or eschew them altogether. Talking heads on television will have respectful and nuanced debates about how best to support all people without vilifying black, single mothers as "welfare queens." And "family values," already noxious and evacuated of any productive meaning from the moment it arrived in political discourse, will have become completely unintelligible. Family, what is that? Which one?

And me and my Ts might move into that house, but maybe not. Maybe we'll grow attached to this mediating half block; maybe I'll want to close the door on those friends and lovers from time to time. When the mold of the model family is finally and fully discarded, maybe that desire for a shared brood of children will evaporate. But we won't laugh when we remember it.

Sam Huber *is a writer and editor living in Brooklyn, New York, with or near T1, T2, C1, C2, E, A, L, and S.*

Let Him Wear a Tutu

YAMBERLIE M. TAVAREZ

Standing barefoot in the kitchen, with rollers in my hair, a baby clutching my hip, I scramble up these eggs. My husband is thrown across the couch, grasping tightly at his ball sack. God forbid they run away!

What a life to be domesticated. Where is my diploma now? My dreams, wants, aspirations? Oh right, I watch them as they slowly trickle down the sink, with the grease scrubbed off these pots and pans.

And now that I've been put "in my place," they've moved on to my son.

Others look at him and say, *You haven't cut his hair? You know he'll be confused. Kids in his class will tease. They'll say that he's a girl! You're being stubborn Yam, just to prove your point.* But I love my baby's hair, his long gorgeous locks brushing across his face, his pretty little face.

I say: Let him wear a tutu. Let her wear a cape! Yes, yes he is a boy. And yes, you see his hair *is* long. Let him wear a ponytail, a purple ribbon in his hair. Screw it, let him paint his nails with pink polka dots if he truly wants. So what her hair won't grow? Who cares if she won't wear a skirt, let her wear a bow tie instead, let her uncross her legs, and screw it, let her date! Someone please explain to me why it's such a problem, what's the big freaking deal?

Let us deconstruct these mindsets, wrapped in blankets of expectations, blankets of pink or blue. We'll focus on the new seeds we plant in the younger minds. Break through the conditioning. Raise a new generation without forced gender, that ridiculous preoccupation. Build them up without cutting them down; giving them options rather than stripping their minds.

Let the boys join gymnastics, prance around in ballet. Let the girls do karate. Let them have a brain!

I'll tell Ryan it's okay to cry. Because boys do have feelings, just like girls can be strong. I'll tell my nieces to speak their mind, cheer when they play softball, go wild when they question life, question the world, ask "why not?" I'll tell them that they're not these fragile princesses, more than damsels in distress, bigger than fairy tale seekers, greater than a sidepiece to some royal prick!

Here's what I propose we do to create this feminist utopia: let's liberate ourselves from gendered expectations while our babies are still in the womb. Let's take away the "big reveal." Bring them into a blank space. Allow them to choose their own colors, decide their own ways. What knowledge does this creature have of gender's rulebook before being expelled from your body, thrust into this cold world of he's and she's, of him and her?

Oh, and here's a brilliant idea: How about a baby shower to celebrate a *life*? A celebration without cheesy themes and gender classifications. A shower with a rainbow, all possible colors, fuchsia, blue, aquamarine, yellow, gold, olive, black, blue, salmon, teal, and light coral.

Paint the baby room a color without knowing for whom.

Be grateful that your child is born, that this little person exists. Don't stress about if it's that boy you wanted or, *oops*, you got a girl. It is yours, alive and well. Embrace this little being, hold it tight in your arms and close to your heart.

A penis? Vagina? What will the doctor pronounce? How about they simply say, "Congratulations, a human being! You did a great job!" You can tell your friends, put up Facebook posts, you can still be proud, but instead of it's a girl, rather than it's a boy, just state how full of joy you are that you made this precious child.

Name her Xavier-Francois. His name could be Penelope Delilah. Names can be chosen because you simply like the sound.

Though yes, in my son's life, he already has a boy's name and the baby-shower balloons were blue and he does have tons and tons of toy cars and his favorite color is blue (and my favorite color just happens to be pink) . . . but I can still imagine this utopia.

In this utopia we say: Let him wear a tutu. Let her wear a cape! Yes, yes he is a boy. And yes, you see his hair *is* long. Let him wear a ponytail, a purple ribbon in his hair. Screw it, let him paint his nails with pink polka dots if he truly wants. So what her hair won't grow? Who cares if she won't wear a skirt, let her wear a bow tie instead, let her uncross her legs, and screw it, let her date! Someone please explain to me why it's such a problem, what's the big freaking deal . . . Let them eat their fucking cake!

My dreams benefit from youth and inexperience. Of course, you might just question to what lengths, to what extent, my naiveté stretches. Trusting enough to believe that it is possible. Foolish enough to go out and try.

Striving to change the world one less pink blanket and one less can of blue paint at a time.

Yamberlie M. Tavarez *is a New School alumna, with a bachelor's in literary studies. She is mother to a four-year-old spirited little person, Ryan Nathaniel. She is currently attempting to find the mythical work-life balance, and discovering new perspectives along the way. Yamberlie is a New York-born Latina writer, essayist, and poet. Her writing focuses on parenting, gender roles in society, race, and the dynamics of human relationships.*

Interview with Ileana Jiménez

ILLUSTRATION BY RUTH TAM

The following is excerpted from a conversation over email in the fall of 2014 between the editors and Ileana Jiménez, who has been a leader in social justice education for more than eighteen years. In 2009, in an effort to inspire teachers to bring women's studies to the K-12 classroom, she launched her blog, Feminist Teacher, which has a dedicated following among social justice educators, activists, and academics. She is also the creator of the #HSfeminism and #K12feminism hashtags, which have brought visibility to the global movement to introduce feminism to more schools and students. Based in New York, Ileana teaches innovative courses on feminism and activism, and is the 2011 recipient of the Distinguished Fulbright Award in Teaching.

What would students learn in a utopian school?

First, the students and the teachers would build the

school together by designing inclusive curricula, implementing national and global programs, collaborating with students and teachers in other schools, and writing and speaking for public audiences beyond the classroom. From kindergarten through high school, students and teachers would create schools that reflect the needs of the communities they are in.

In a utopia, what we now learn in separate women's, gender, queer, and ethnic studies classes in college would be integrated across the K-12 curriculum. Learning would be interdisciplinary, project- and passion-based, rather than separated into discreet content areas that don't seem to speak to each other or to our students. A feminist, queer, and antiracist approach would be applied to everything from reading novels, to doing a lab, to learning a language, to learning how to be in healthy relationships.

Students would not have to take tests or exams. Instead, we would engage students in problem solving to sustain the utopia they live in. Students would design projects that put into practice what they have learned that can be shared with others, including local and national leaders. A video about preventing intimate partner violence. A website about Latina women in history. A collaborative project with students in another country on sustaining peace.

The school's curriculum would ultimately aim at honoring multiple heritages across the world, nurturing present-day communities, and dismantling destructive

power structures that lead to violence both in and out of our homes.

Why would a feminist education in K-12 schools sustain a utopia?

When I was in first grade in the early eighties, my family moved from the Bronx to Long Island, and I was frequently called the n-word, "Afro," "Spic," and "lesbian" by children on the playground. Some people call this bullying. But at heart, it's a form of violence. Bullying and harassment stem from racism and sexism, homophobia and transphobia. A feminist education is about stopping this kind of ignorance and violence so that we can cultivate compassion and love instead.

So, what if the goal of a feminist school was to teach young people to love? Wouldn't that be the ultimate goal of a utopia? To live in a loving world? And wouldn't schools be the first place where we could teach these skills to help sustain the utopia we want to live in?

Children and teens—both white and of color—who learn the histories and stories of all marginalized groups *and* who also become aware of destructive messages about race, class, gender, and sexuality, become that much more sensitive to and caring about each other and the world around them. The goal is not to become blind to difference. Instead, young people will know that racism, sexism, classism, homophobia, and transphobia do exist, and will work everyday to end these oppressions. In a utopia, they will work everyday to help prevent them from coming back. That's the goal.

If my elementary school teachers had been provided the training to teach an antiracist curriculum that was inclusive of all of the cultures of the children in my class, I might not have been bullied for being a curly-haired Puerto Rican girl. Indeed, I might not have internalized from a very young age that being Puerto Rican was somehow wrong. It might not have taken me until college to learn the language that named the pain I had gone through as a child.

How would teachers be treated differently in a utopia?

We'd stop bullying teachers. Administrators, politicians, and the media would start treating us as thought leaders and as public intellectuals, and would turn to us to teach them how to craft equitable education policies and how to govern our schools from within instead of from without. They would realize that most of us teachers are women and that, in keeping with the history of under-compensated women's labor, we have hardly been paid to survive let alone thrive. Higher salaries that reflect our actual intellectual and emotional labor would elevate not only our profession but also our collective morale.

Equally important, the workday would reflect teacher interests as much as student interests. Teachers are expected to cultivate the intellectual lives of young people and yet we are not supported to cultivate our own. In my utopia, teachers would have time to do research, write articles, speak to the media, and shape community concerns not only locally but also nationally and globally. They would have enough money to travel around the world, collaborating with other teachers and students, imagining and creating new possibilities for young people and themselves.

You teach students around the world. Would utopian education be internationally minded?

Yes, absolutely. One thing that I have learned in working with students from Mexico to India to the UK, is that they are all hungry for these kinds of conversations. Globally, young people are baffled as to why they are so censored and regulated at school. They are the first ones to testify that they want to break down the prescribed gender roles reified by school rules. They also want to be able to know that they will be allowed to love someone, regardless of their gender. They want real sex education. They want to know the histories and cultures of their peers in other countries. They want an education—not some imperialist, colonial remnant of the past.

If we were more global and feminist in our education practices, we would be able to end patriarchy as it exists. If we learned more about the world as children and as teenagers and if we were able to travel not as consuming tourists but as compassionate learners, we would not become war-mongering, we would not become power-hungry, and we would not become so hateful to and dominating of one another.

More than anything, young people want to be connected with each other. We live in an exciting time to make this happen. I just recently invited a group of students from Delhi who started the first GSA [Gay Straight Alliance] in India to talk with the students in my high school feminism class in New York. Their group is called Breaking Barriers and I met these students during a guest teaching tour of schools I did in India in early 2014. After my time in India, I invited Breaking Barriers to visit my high school feminism class, which is made up of a diverse group of juniors and seniors who identify as African American, Latino, Indian, Bangladeshi, and white. They were able to have face-to-face conversations with each other about how to be advocates and activists on behalf of issues that matter to them, such as supporting queer youth or stopping gender-based violence or ending racism.

These students will continue to be engaged with each other beyond the confines of classes and grades and school trips. While social media will certainly keep them connected, it will actually be their common desire to change the world that will inspire long-term partnerships. Out of those partnerships, they will be inspired to design innovative platforms and on-the-ground projects that will lead us to the very utopia we are talking about. I imagine them finding each other at future conferences and summits, sharing new ideas about how to sustain the world they helped to change.

I'll be right there with them.

Ruth Tam *is a web producer at DC's NPR affiliate, WAMU. She has written and illustrated for the* Washington Post, PBS NewsHour, *and* Global Post. *She lives in Washington, DC, where she enjoys cheese, beer, and talking to strangers.*

Interview with Cindy Ok

The following is excerpted from an interview an editor conducted with Cindy Ok, a public high school teacher in Los Angeles, over the phone on February 2, 2015. Just one year out of college, Ok teaches physics, computer science, and math to roughly two hundred students per day in seven different classes, so we were eager to talk with her about the logistics of organizing a classroom in a feminist utopia.

How would classrooms be arranged in a feminist utopia?

In a feminist utopia, a lot of learning would happen through exploring outside, and indoor spaces would encourage interaction between students. I am intellectually and viscerally against static rows, where students are separated from one another and face the teacher. I prefer circles and pods—little groups of tables—so students can face each other.

This form promotes equality because the classroom centers on the students, rather than positioning the teacher as the focus, while the students look up at him or her. And rather than positioning the teacher as this giver of information and the students as the receivers of information, students have social contact and learn from one another. A dynamic setup sees students as complex, perceptive, and knowledgeable. It allows them to bring their identities and lived experiences into the classroom rather than sit in rows like robots, memorizing whatever the person at the front is saying and accepting it as true. It empowers them to discover on their own. That's about agency. That's feminist.

How would that ethos manifest itself in classroom lessons?

The way teaching works now in most public schools is really industrial—a cost/benefit analysis, a goal of efficiency. There should be a radically active relationship between people and learning, a lot more projects and student-run lessons that are truly interdisciplinary and significant. So many artificial boundaries between subjects and disciplines would be bridged. No question would ever be dismissed as "not part of the lesson" or "for a different class," because the driving values would be curiosity, self-honesty, and self-knowledge, and this broader common good: equity. We would value process over product.

So, for example, we could teach reproductive health totally differently. Maybe a student would present a history of abortion access in America by interviewing her grandparents and older neighbors about their experiences. Students would be reading personal, cultural, and political narratives about abortion early on and continuously, not in a "chapter" on abortion but as a by-product of art reflecting life in the utopia.

This kind of education around reproductive justice would be multidisciplinary. Reproductive health would not be cloaked in shame and secrecy and euphemisms, and so students could openly learn about the science behind it all. They would work with pharmacists to study the compounding process behind birth control. And of course they'd be learning about reproductive health in the utopian versions of health classes, which would include knowledge about all the accessible and valuable birth control options (most of which we can only dream of), and explore the statistical and medical realities surrounding abortion. Throughout their education, through books, conversations, interviews, reviews, and visits, they build an understanding and an idea that is whole; that brings together the parts as intimately linked and in a way that acknowledges the history and politics of reproductive health.

The fact that all classes—whether it's health or science or history or literature—are feminist and antiracist would be implicitly acknowledged by doing away with "electives" for gender studies or Chicano studies, or even having a section of US history for "African American history" as though it's separate from the rest of American history.

Lessons would be flexible to student need and student interest. For example, this week one of my students took me up on a trigger warning, and I gave her an alternative assignment—a project that covered the same content in about the same amount of time. And then I just realized I could give both options at the beginning of class, to everyone. And it's a similar key with my students who have special needs or are learning English. To make things accessible, I'll have guided notes or vocabulary organizers. It's clear that these should be options for everyone. Those that don't need or want them, then great, but we can all benefit from that act of choice.

How would this more holistic vision of students change how kids learn?

Classrooms can't be neutral. Just like in journalism or in law or in medicine, there's no such thing as objectivity in an absolute sense. Any decision you make as a teacher affects the students and to some degree reveals assumptions you have about them. Whether or not you tell them about your family sets a tone; whether or not you display student work or photos or goals tells them something about how you will use your position of power. Trying to force a student to be a blank slate, coming into the physics classroom in this singular role as a physics student, takes away from the potential of the classroom as community. If they're people, if they feel like and are treated as the inconsistent and thoughtful and complicated people they are, the class can learn more from one another.

I'm thinking about the ways my female students are taught to think about science and math, and I think these utopian strategies give equal opportunities super early on. I keep thinking about my students who are sixteen, seventeen, eighteen, nineteen years old, and wondering what it would be like had they had all these opportunities from infancy, if for all those years girls were raising their hands and getting called on as much as the boys. If women came into the world with the same expectations as men—the same resources, the same championship—the science and professional worlds would of course be more diverse. We would see the same level of confidence and success with women, people who are nonbinary, people of color, people with different abilities—all across the board.

Learning Our Bodies, Healing Our Selves

WILLIAM SCHLESINGER

Historically, biological science has been employed to buttress the notion that women are physically and mentally inferior to men, that people of color are of subordinate intelligence and disposed to criminality and poverty, that gender nonnormativity is a psychological disorder, and that same-sex desire is rooted in genetic aberration. Sexism, racism, transphobia, and homophobia have found in science an all-too-willing lackey. When called on to protect and validate the dominance of straight, white, cisgender men, science has demonstrated its capacity to make oppression and injustice appear justifiable, and even worse, natural. The fact that the medical and scientific communities in the United States have been traditionally composed of white men of privilege should come as no surprise.

And because science is in the business of making

sense, we can easily become convinced that the pursuit of scientific knowledge will lead us to gradually uncover naturally existing, unifying truths about the world. We can easily forget that scientists do not simply uncover truths—they are complicit in creating truths.

Medicine involves the translation of these situated scientific principles into the care and treatment of our bodies. The conclusions drawn from science are implemented through medical discourse and practice in ways that exert a very material impact. But if we were able to fully appreciate that knowledge produced in the biological sciences is not only about chromosomes and hormones but also about identities and subjectivities, the field of medicine would be transformed.

What would health care look like if the practice of medicine were vocally and unequivocally oriented toward the fulfillment of feminist goals? My experience as a premedical student has convinced me that for access to this reality, we'd need to start over with the education of future physicians.

How might the premedical classroom—an early and formative station in the development of the next generation of physicians—serve as a staging ground for a significant shift toward feminist politics in the principles, priorities, and practices associated with health care and healing?

A trip to a premed biology course illustrates a major hurdle. Biology as is currently taught to premeds is deeply invested in the doctrine of sexual dimorphism—the identification of phenotypic differences between "biological males" and "biological females"—as an explanatory framework. At every step, students are taught how male and female bodies are different, from bones down to hormones. Stereotypes about masculinity and femininity permeate the messaging of biology so thoroughly, that, as anthropologist Emily Martin famously pointed out, we internalize the narrative of the intrepid, active sperm engaged in heroic competition to penetrate the dormant, docile egg.

Passing this fixation down to the next generation of medical practitioners only serves to anchor the continual reinscription of a dichotomy between "men" and "women," propping up sexism and patriarchy. The naturalization of sexual difference through medical discourse continues to represent inequality as inborn fact.

In my feminist utopia, we've stopped searching for the translocated chromosomal region that may or may not help answer some part of the question, "What's the relationship between biology and sexual desire or gender identity?" We've stopped not only because we understand how flawed the question is, but also because our scientific focus has shifted entirely. In my feminist utopia, we're searching for the best ways to care for those whose identities have been pathologized, and whose health and life quality has been systematically undervalued. Science will not focus on explaining away our questions, but rather push us to ask the most pressing ones at the forefront of care, beginning with: "Where are we needed?"

This attitude certainly exists among individual physicians, medical anthropologists, public health professionals, social workers, health advocates, and activists of many stripes. This kind of thinking is already reflected to varying degrees in the missions of certain health-focused organizations. But what would happen if using health care as a vehicle for social justice were to be adopted as *the core* commitment of premedical and medical education?

In my feminist utopia, premedical education would be designed to instill an understanding that health care inequality and the unequal distribution of life chances are not genetically programmed inevitabilities, but rather the result of structural oppression. The history and legacy of sexist, racist, homophobic, and colonial medicine would necessarily be a centerpiece of this curriculum. The doctors trained in these programs would learn to recognize their own careers as opportunities to work toward keeping these circumstances in the pre-utopian past. But they would also be taught that efforts made with ostensibly good intentions don't always necessarily translate into an unambiguously positive result. To achieve this understanding, medical education would be far more interdisciplinary, with students taking courses that expose them to critiques of medicine as a site of violence. Classes in medical anthropology would demonstrate the reality that medical knowledge can pathologize, and that ignorant interventions can kill. Work in gender studies and comparative ethnic studies would help connect the social and biological dimensions of health.

As doctors trained in these programs started to populate hospitals and clinics across the country, the practice of medicine would open itself up increasingly to knowledges that are currently considered tangential or out of scope. The borders that medicine has constructed around the body as its sole domain would start to dissolve. Differing knowledges around health and the body would not compete for legitimacy, but would rather reinforce one another. The gap between "modern" biomedicine and traditional or folk remedies would be bridged in the effort to create a multivocal, diverse body of healers.

These changes would, of course, be precipitated by a sweeping change in the economics behind medical training and health care in general. Premedical education would be free, so that graduating students would be able to select their specialty without consideration for how to most expediently repay hundreds of thousands of dollars of accrued debt. This alone might make the shortage in primary care practitioners disappear, and would also radically change the demographics in the field.

Without financial barriers to a medical education,

the profile of the typical medical student would change drastically. Currently, even the application process can be prohibitively expensive. According to statistics released by the Association of American Medical Colleges (AAMC), the average medical school hopeful submits fourteen applications in a given admissions cycle, which, with application and MCAT fees alone, easily costs upwards of $2,000. Those who are lucky enough to win a coveted interview spot can expect to pay their own travel and lodging expenses —if they can take the time off from work for multiple, short-notice trips! In a feminist utopia, these financial barriers to a medical education would be unthinkable. As a result, the next generation of physicians would include significantly more doctors who had experienced living in medically underserved areas themselves, which would help keep the priorities of the entire medical community in line with material reality.

Access to health care would be considered a fundamental right. Nothing could help bring us closer to our utopian goal than the guaranteed provision of quality health care to all, regardless of gender identity, race, sexuality, income, or citizenship status. Part of maintaining the unequal power relationships that underpin oppression is that certain bodies are allowed to die, while others are kept alive. In a context permeated with violence against nonnormative bodies, survival is political, but it shouldn't be. To reach and protect a feminist utopia, medical education would be geared toward preparing students to best address the needs of those who suffer most: if our doctors always rush to pick up those most in need, we won't leave anyone behind. To preserve the equality achieved in that utopia, doctors would have to keep this priority central to their practice. We'll need to work actively to make sure we don't slip back.

In a future where every medical student in the country receiving their diplomas is entering the field with a commitment to doing that work, the power of science and medicine will be channeled toward liberation.

William Schlesinger *completed a Fulbright fellowship in the politics of HIV/AIDS, immigration, and integration in Germany. In the future, he hopes to pursue an MD/PhD in medical anthropology to combine practicing medicine as a primary care physician while conducting ethnographic research on health inequalities.*

Feminist Utopia Teen Mom Schedule

GLORIA MALONE

6:00 a.m. Sophia wakes up, eats breakfast, pumps breast milk for the day, takes a shower, and wakes up the baby.

6:30 a.m. She changes the baby's diaper, feeds the baby, plays with her for a little bit, then Sophia's father takes the baby so Sophia can double-check her backpack and her daughter's diaper bag.

6:55 a.m. There's a quick emergency diaper change before putting the car seat in Sophia's car, loading the diaper bag and her backpack into the car, and leaving for the childcare center.

7:00 a.m. Before pulling out of the driveway, Sophia looks down at the gas gauge on her car. She sends her mother a thank-you text message for topping off her gas tank without her asking or knowing. She no longer has to stop at the gas station during morning rush hour.

7:15 a.m. Sophia arrives at her friend Naomi's house to pick Naomi and her son up so they can ride to school together.

7:45 a.m. Sophia, Naomi, and their children arrive at the high school's on-campus childcare center. They unload the car, walk inside, and are greeted by the friendly staff of the facility.

"Hi!" the front desk clerk says when the girls walk in. Sophia's daughter and Naomi's son begin cooing and smiling when they hear the familiar voices of the friendly, knowledgeable, and loving staff that takes care of them while their mothers are at school.

7:50 a.m. The mothers walk into their children's clean, bright, and safe day-care room where they spend the next ten minutes talking and breast-feeding their children, without being obligated to cover up, while the staff puts the morning's freshly pumped breast milk into the center's refrigerator.

8:00 a.m. Sophia and Naomi say goodbye to their children and walk over to their high school's courtyard where they meet up with their other friends. The girls talk with their friends about life, annoying teachers, their plans for the weekend, and the latest episode of their favorite show.

8:15 a.m. Sophia goes to her first-period class, art history.

8:45 a.m. During class, Sophia feels her cell phone vibrate and checks her text messages. She opens the message from her daughter's teacher to find a photo of her daughter playing with her friends at the child-care center and a message that reads, "Have a great day mommy I love you."

9:15 a.m. Sophia meets with her Title IX coordinator who wants to check in to make sure all of her teachers and the staff and faculty of the school are being mindful of Sophia's federal rights to continue her education as a parenting student. After the formalities, the two talk about Sophia's daughter's milestones, the wonderful on-site childcare facility, and whether Sophia will be going to the high school's homecoming sporting events. Sophia replies that her parents have agreed to watch her daughter so she can go to the games with a few of her friends.

9:40 a.m. Sophia walks in a few minutes late to her second-period class. Her teacher gives her a little nod showing her not to worry that she was late.

11:20 a.m. Sophia's class is dismissed. She makes her way over to the lactation room on campus that faculty, staff, and students alike use to breast-feed their children or pump their breast milk.

11:25 a.m. In the lactation room, Sophia and the other people inside start sharing tips on the best nipple balms, how to avoid nipple cracking, and how to modify their supply, and talk about the upcoming homecoming festivities.

Because Sophia ate her lunch in the lactation room, she decides to spend half her time in the lunchroom with her friends and the rest of the school's allocated free hour to visit her daughter and drop off her new supply of breast milk.

12:05 p.m. After the baby falls asleep and Sophia has to stop herself from doing the same, she lays her daughter down in her crib, kisses her goodbye, and rushes across campus to her fourth-period class.

2:50 p.m. School is dismissed. Sophia walks with her friends for a bit. They ask her about the baby, and she responds that things are great.

3:00 p.m. Sophia arrives at the childcare center, where she is greeted by a smiling, happy baby and, to her surprise, her mother. "Thank you for topping off my gas tank," she tells her mother. "You're welcome, honey. I wanted to help you out a little bit." Sophia breast-feeds her daughter before they get ready to leave.

She gets a text message from Naomi: "I have drama club after school today. My son's dad will be picking him up so we don't need a ride. Thanks."

3:15 p.m. Sophia, her daughter, and her friend Jeffrey, a single teenage father who is one of Sophia's friends, make their way over to the local bookstore for Read to Me story hour with their children.

4:00 p.m. Read to Me story hour starts. Sophia and her daughter and Jeffrey and his daughter sit on the designated bookstore rugs and listen to a very animated storytelling of *The Cat in the Hat*.

4:45 p.m. They leave the bookstore. Jeffrey and Sophia say goodbye to one another and go their separate ways to their homes.

5:00 p.m. Sophia and her daughter arrive at home. Sophia's father has cooked dinner and takes care of the baby while Sophia eats.

5:10 p.m. Sophia finishes eating and then begins to read the chapters of one of her homework assignments while breast-feeding her daughter.

5:30 p.m. Sophia and her daughter play on the floor while Sophia sneaks in some more reading.

6:30 p.m. The baby starts getting a bit cranky and Sophia decides to start getting things ready for bath time.

7:00 p.m. The baby is washed, fed, and tucked into her crib.

7:30 p.m. Sophia's daughter has fallen asleep and Sophia starts on her other homework assignments.

8:00 p.m. Sophia's sister gets home and they get ready to watch their favorite show together.

9:40 p.m. Sophia finishes the rest of her homework after having to lull the baby back to sleep after she woke up crying.

11:30 p.m. Sophia falls asleep. As she falls asleep, she begins to reflect on her life. Although she is very tired and looks forward to the time when her daughter can sleep all through the night, she is happy, healthy, and grateful that she lives in a society that is helpful and uplifting of her and her family.

2:00 a.m. She wakes up to her daughter crying. She checks her diaper, feeds her, and the two fall back asleep.

6:00 a.m. Sophia wakes and gets ready for the day.

Gloria Malone *is a writer and reproductive justice advocate. Her works exist at the intersections of race, socioeconomic class, and living a life free of respectability politics. You can find her on Twitter @GloriaMalone.*

New Rites of Transition

GABRIELLE GAMBOA

Gabrielle Gamboa *is a visual artist and arts educator who lives in Santa Rosa, California. Her comics and illustrations have appeared in print and online publications such as* Salon, BUST, *and* Truthout. *She is currently working on a graphic novel set in postwar Los Angeles.*

Before
going
out into the world,

each young woman
is fitted with a
suit of armor.

This shields
her from
the judgement
of those
who believe
her intrinsic
value is
her looks.

It renders her immune
to those who wish
to control her body.

This armor grows and changes with her.

She is given a sharp, quick sword,

to cut through her fears of being made an outcast for her ambition.

To banish the inner demons who only want her to placate, to just be "a good sport."

She is also given a cell phone containing the numbers of marvelous mentors she can call at any time.

Finally,

She is crowned with a grand plumed helm.

This will ensure that she will never be tempted to make herself small or unseen.

She will always be heard.

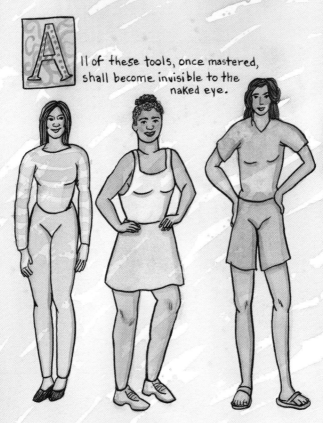

All of these tools, once mastered, shall become invisible to the naked eye.

But with her always.

Renouncing Reality

CHANELLE ADAMS

Chanelle Adams *is a multiracial, forever multitasking writer/artist/scientist/historian interested in multiplicities, borders, cognitive justice, and systems of knowledge production. When she's not talking to you about "the core issues" at inappropriate times, she's at home wearing velvet and zine-ing. She is currently a student in the Science & Technology Studies (STS) program at Brown University and editor in chief of* Bluestockings *magazine.*

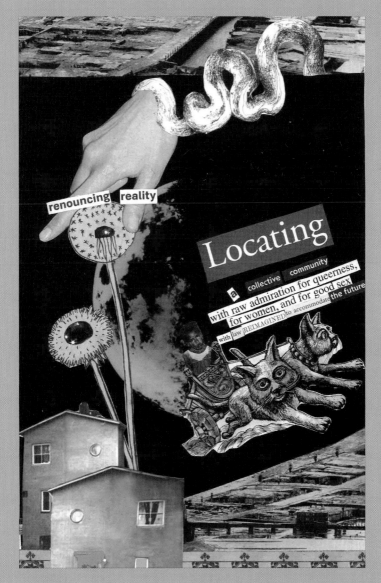

renouncing reality

Locating

a collective community

with raw admiration for queerness, for women, and for good sex

with law REIMAGINED to accommodate the future

What Will Children Play with in Utopia?

Or: What Is the Opposite of a Mirror?

KATE RILEY
ILLUSTRATIONS BY RICHARD ESPINOSA

Measure the sickness of a society by how frequently its children see their own reflections—in surfaces, photographs, PhotoBooth, iPad screens, and, subtly but relentlessly, in software designed to learn, replicate, and reinforce their behavior. A vicious cycle of self-surveillance narrows experience until there is no self left to reflect. In its place, merely the frantic scramble for confirmation of existence: I am that I look in the mirror.

We cannot deny or attack the narcotic effect of the reflection, but must instead give children objects that deflect self-absorption, and encourage humble reverence for the world. Objects that by their very nature instruct physicality, messiness, and impermanence.

What is the opposite of a mirror? Mud absorbs light, coating and deleting everything it touches. Wet sand, yeasted dough, caterpillars, and bubble-wrap all teach through touch. And the true opposite of a mirror, another human face, contains and represents all any child needs to learn: that other people are.

Kate Riley *looks after children in New York City.*

Richard Espinosa *is from New Jersey and is currently a student at the Yale School of Art studying graphic design. Richard is the current director of YAMP—the Yale AIDS Memorial Project, a localized narrative-based alumni-led initiative to honor the lives of the deceased students, faculty and staff affiliated with Yale. Richard also works for the Yale Dean's Office at both the Alcohol and Other Drug Harm Reduction Initiative and the Office of Gender and Campus Culture, and is a student fellow at the Global Health Justice Partnership.*

DOUGH

DEFLECT SELF-ABSORPTION

2+

ENCOURAGE HUMBLE REVERENCE

4+

WET
SAND

AND MUD

8+

BUBBLE
WRAP

AND CATERPILLARS

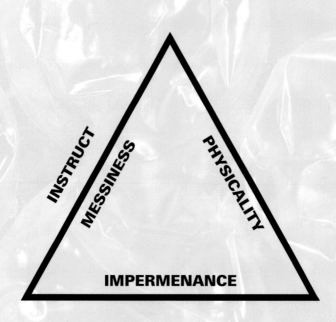

INSTRUCT

MESSINESS

PHYSICALITY

IMPERMENANCE

Back to School 1 and 2

TYLER COHEN

Tyler Cohen *is a cartoonist who works with multiple voices: surrealism, true vignettes, and journalistic bits about language. She mixes all three in the* Primahood *comic books—an emotional journey through being a feminist mother of a young daughter and an engagement with questions as to what is female. Her work has been published in QU33R, from Northwest Press, and on Mutha Magazine online. Forthcoming is a collaboration with her sister (the writer Kerry Cohen) about female friendships (mostly the bad ones) from childhood to adulthood— coming in 2015 from Hawthorne Books. Tyler Cohen lives in San Francisco and works as a freelance artist, teacher, and designer. You can find her work at primazonia.com and tylerzonia.tumblr.com.*

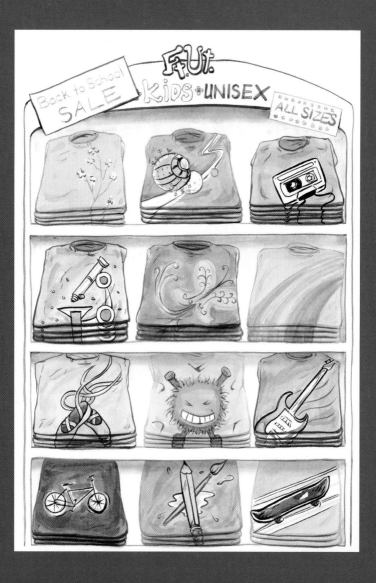

Not a Favor to Women

The Workplace in a Feminist Future

ELLEN BRAVO

Anna couldn't hold her head up. She'd known what Mr. Luchsinger would say when she tried to call in sick: "If you don't come in, don't come back."

The rent was overdue and the baby needed a new inhaler. So Anna dragged herself in to Klondike Pharmaceuticals. But between the sinus infection and the chemicals in the floor wax, she couldn't help curling up on the rag pile in the janitors' supply closet—really, she just meant to take five.

When Anna awoke and pushed open the closet door, the first thing she noticed was the scent. Instead of the harsh chemicals that left her throat too raw to swallow, the air smelled fresh, like that park with the willow trees where her dad took her one Sunday.

The next thing she noticed was the calendar: March 8, 2063. Whose idea of a joke was this?

Two women were wheeling a cart down the hall. One side sported shiny chartreuse letters that read: "Green and Clean Co-Op." Instead of the drab gray uniform Anna was wearing—her coworker Jerome called it "prison garb"—these women were decked out in bright colors. Neither looked familiar.

"Hey," Anna said. "Did Luchsinger bring you in from another shop?"

"Who's Luchsinger?" The woman who asked had silver hair, but she looked really strong and fit.

"Head honcho for Lux Cleaners."

The older woman turned to her coworker, who appeared to be in her late twenties and four or five months pregnant. "We read about them last month in our history circle. Fifty years ago, they had the maintenance contract here."

"Hey, *chica*," the other woman said to Anna. "I'm Silvia and this is Marion. Come to the break room with us. You look like you just saw a ghost."

The two led Anna to a spacious room at the end of the floor. Inside were clusters of people talking and laughing. Anna didn't know which was more surprising—the number of women in lab coats, the realization that most weren't Caucasian, or the fact that scientists and custodians sat at the same tables. Colorful paintings covered the walls. She heard unmistakable toddler squeals next door.

Marion took her elbow and led her to a round table in the corner. "I read about other cases just like yours," Marion said. "What year did you fall asleep?"

If this was a dream, Anna didn't want to wake up.

"2013."

Silvia grinned and pointed to the nametag hanging around Anna's neck. "Welcome, Anna. You can take that off. Everyone here learns each other's name at our weekly get-togethers."

No one but the other janitors had ever known Anna's name. She'd often wondered if the scientists even saw her.

Marion crossed the room to a long table stacked with food and brought back a plate of salad and a tall glass of water. Anna fumbled in her pocket for her change purse.

"There hasn't been a charge for lunch in thirty years," Marion said as she took her seat. "So, you must have been here when the company got caught in that scandal."

Anna nodded. Klondike Pharmaceuticals was charged with hiding a study that showed its famous—and highly profitable—diabetes drug caused damaging side effects.

"Those days are gone," Marion said. "Each team takes responsibility for quality control; it's part of their assessment portfolio."

"What about the cost?" Anna pictured her cousin, skeletal from AIDS. No miracle drugs for the uninsured.

Marion drew their attention to a poster on the wall. "Ever since Congress passed Medicare for All, the cost of drugs is minimal. The government subsidizes research. You remember all those lobbyists Klondike used to hire?"

"What's a lobbyist?" Silvia asked.

Marion explained how giant corporations spent millions on people whose job was to pad campaign funds and distribute so-called studies that proved whatever the lobbyists were pushing was necessary and beneficial.

"Suits," Anna said. "That's what we called them," shivering as she remembered one who asked for directions while pinning her against the wall. "What happened to those guys?"

Marion threw her head back and laughed. "Look at the display in the library. That's one of the few job categories that's plummeted in the last decade."

A library! Anna couldn't believe it.

"I can't imagine how you folks survived," Silvia said. Her hand moved to the soft swell of her belly under her tunic. "The history team told us all about it last month—how custodial workers were hired by a subcontractor, shifts were always changing, piss poor pay, no benefits, having to work sick—unbelievable."

"The history team?"

"Oh, you can participate in all sorts of teams," Marion said. "We have the usual: history, culture, music, art." She pointed to the walls. "That's who picks out the paintings we purchase."

"We." Anna rolled the word around on her tongue like a delicacy. "But none of the people I knew had time to be on a team."

Now it was Silvia's turn to let out a lovely peal of laughter. "That's because you worked your butt off, sister. Since the workweek was reduced to thirty hours, we all have lots more time to do things we love."

"Sometimes team members lead on-the-job training

sessions," Marion added. "Like Damien and Sharla—they did a series on the history of racial injustice. Or someone might lead a language class."

"You mean for immigrants who want to learn English?" Anna asked.

"Sometimes," Marion said. "But people today move pretty freely between borders. So mainly the classes are for those who want to learn new languages—mostly Spanish, maybe a little Greek or Swahili before your sabbatical."

Anna almost choked on her beets as they described the sabbatical available after seven years.

"How can you pay your rent with only thirty hours a week?" she asked.

"Oh, that's full-time pay," Silvia said. "The way we work, everyone is more efficient. No surprise—rested workers do a better job. Virtually everyone who wants to be is employed. And most people own homes. "

While Anna finished her salad, Silvia explained how the unions worked with managers to set up a series of co-ops for all the nonscientific functions in the workplace. Workers were actually owners of their sections and made all the decisions.

"Next you're going to tell me everyone makes the same pay and there's no have's and have not's," said Anna.

"There are plenty of have's," Marion said. "But thanks to the changes in the laws, tax dollars no longer get sucked into corporate welfare. And they also aren't needed for stuff like food stamps—not since we passed the thriveable wage law. The co-ops all have seats on corporate boards, so that keeps the top-pay in line. At most it's no more than twenty times the average worker's wage."

Anna pointed at a group of women scientists. "There used to be so few women here," she said. "How did this happen?"

Marion ticked off the reasons on her fingers: "The government enforced the laws. Added new ones. Companies have to conduct an annual audit to see who gets promoted and why. All co-ops set pay rates based on union-management surveys. The Fair Pay Act pretty much removed gender and race bias from compensation. People get raises by improving their skills. Those two scientists over there? One woman started in our co-op, the other in data services."

Anna couldn't stop staring.

"But the biggest change came from protections to value families."

"You mean things like paid sick days and family leave?" Anna remembered reading about a coalition in her city that was working on that.

Silvia walked her over to the bulletin board, jam-packed with pictures of babies and toddlers—but also workers with parents and partners and siblings.

"We finally caught up with the rest of the world," Silvia said. "My wife Alma and I will share sixteen months of leave. Since I'm the one giving birth, I also have four weeks off before the baby is due. Alma's a teacher, so her coteacher will mentor a new person during the semester she's off. I'll come back part-time at first, and I'll bring the baby."

"We've had part-time equity since 2018," Marion explained, "and that includes advancement as well as pay. The three management team leaders—what you all called a CEO?—include two women. One was hired when she was pregnant. And the guy took six months for each of his two kids."

They walked Anna to the lactation suite next door to the childcare center and peeked in. Soft music surrounded the occupants, mostly seated in recliners, a few in cedar rocking chairs, the others curled up on a love seat.

Anna remembered having to leave—and wean—Alicia when she was only four weeks old. "Wow," she said. "What about guys? Do they actually take leave?"

Marion put her hands on her hips. "Oh, yeah. They have to take at least six months or the family loses the time. But now that the FAMLI fund—that's what we call Family and Medical Leave Insurance—covers 85 percent of pay, most men want to take the leave. This place—most employers, really—pick up the salary difference. The men are loving it. Look at the childcare center—since that became a good job, nearly half the staff are male."

Anna took in the men stacking blocks and painting with the toddlers next door.

"Back when my kids were born, we got only twelve weeks," Marion said, "none of it paid. My husband Jamal took four weeks—we almost lost our house. Last year he took four months of FAMLI leave to be with his dad after he had a stroke. Didn't make a dent in our savings. And you should see my father-in-law now, back on the dance floor. The doctor said Jamal being there in those early months made the difference. Plus the home health care his dad had was amazing."

Anna's best friend worked in home health care. Ai-jen loved her work, but she was always worrying about how to keep the lights on and never could afford to fix her car. What she'd have given to see the day when this was a good job with—what did Marion call it?—a thriveable wage.

"Don't forget the leadership circles," Silvia said. "You want to advance, you got to work hard and have talent. But they also look at how well you can motivate . . . "

"How well you play and work with others!" Marion said.

"If you don't help people integrate work life and personal life," Silvia added, "you'll never get anywhere around here."

Anna shook her head in disbelief. "What did it take to do all this?"

"Good question," Marion said as they walked back. "People realized there were only two ways to go: let the corporate giants keep calling the shots and watch the planet go up in flames, or put the power where it's supposed to be, in the people. Folks kept building coalitions and taking on politicians who were in the pockets of the monied interests. After people power beat money power, they passed new rules that basically took money out of politics. Then we started to win big time—and everything you see followed."

A man with a baby in his arms walked by. Anna felt tears on her cheeks as she thought about Alicia.

"Those other cases, Marion, the people who had fallen asleep—what did they do?"

Marion took Anna's hand in her own. "We have time travel now," she said softly. "You can go back. One of them did—he had young kids, too. Here's the thing: you won't be able to remember any of this. You know, so as not to interfere with history."

Anna swallowed and nodded her head.

"But there is something you'll take back with you," Marion said. "You'll dare to dream the world you know you deserve and you won't settle for anything less. You'll know that change is possible. And you'll know that it's people just like you who will make it happen."

Ellen Bravo *directs the Family Values @ Work Consortium and is the former director of 9to5. Her most recent book is* Taking on the Big Boys: Or Why Feminism Is Good for Families, Business, and the Nation. *She won the Ford Foundation Visionary award and the Francis Perkins Intelligence and Courage award. Ellen lives in Milwaukee with her husband; they have two adult sons.*

Less Work, More Time

MADELEINE SCHWARTZ

It's a cliché of feminist media to bemoan the "time bind" that keeps women tied to the double duties of working and parenting. The solution offered to this problem, however, often boils down to simply working more. "Don't lose sight of your goals!" "Lean in!" As if liberation were the last point on the day's checklist. The question "Can women have it all?" distills decades of frustration and exhaustion into a problem of better scheduling: How can women reconcile an interminable workday with the lion's share of housekeeping and childrearing?

Neither option on its own is desirable; together, they are unbearable. Life shouldn't be reduced to a balance between waged work and housework, a balance between work and work. Instead, if we are concerned about fixing the "time bind," we should do the unimaginable: ask for more time.

The yearly hours of an average worker increased by 181 from 1979 to 2007, according to a 2013 *Economic Policy Institute* report—the equivalent of each working adult taking on an additional 4.5 weeks per year. Meanwhile, wages have stagnated. Extended paid vacation time, even paid maternity leave, is still not available to many Americans. Most work deemed unworthy of pay—childcare and housework—remains primarily women's responsibility and goes uncompensated. These responsibilities add up. The average American woman spends more than two and a half hours a day on house and care work; that's forty-two days of the year consumed by noncompensated efforts.[1] Even kids can't escape the trend of curtailed time. The hours spent on homework have increased 51 percent since 1981.[2]

In response, we might begin to imagine a world without work (or at least much less of it). The proposition for more time has been forcefully articulated by theorist Kathi Weeks in her book *The Problem with Work.* In order to enact this vision, Weeks proposes revisiting the idea of Universal Basic Income. A popular proposal in the 1970s supported by welfare rights workers and, in a reduced form, by the Nixon White House, basic income provides each adult with a fixed sum per year, regardless of whether or not they are employed. This money

1. OECD, "Balancing Paid Work, Unpaid Work and Leisure," July 3, 2014, http://www.oecd.org/gender/data/balancingpaidworkunpaidworkandleisure.htm.
2. F. Thomas Juster, Hiromi Ono, and Frank P. Stafford, "Changing Times of American Youth: 1981–2003," *University of Michigan Institute for Social Research*, November 2004, http://ns.umich.edu/Releases/2004/Nov04/teen_time_report.pdf.

would be distributed equally from the government to all adult citizens on a monthly or yearly basis. It would be unconditional. The amount would not vary on family size or marital status or the recipient's education level or salary.

A basic income would provide a minimum living standard. While not enough to replace a salary, it would begin to eradicate poverty and minimize income inequality. Variations on basic income have been implemented successfully. In Brazil, for example, about a fourth of citizens are covered by the Bolsa Família, a growing program that seeks to provide adults with direct cash transfers. Pilot programs have been implemented in places as varied as Namibia and Manitoba. Indeed, a modified form of basic income already exists in the United States: since 1976, residents of Alaska have received yearly shares of the state's oil revenue. These programs have been shown to improve the quality of life of their participants; in the ten years since Brazil has had Bolsa Família, the number of Brazilians living in poverty has been cut by more than half. The pilot study conducted in Manitoba linked the policy not only with financial well-being but also with increased high school graduation rates and decreased hospitalization. It is perhaps no wonder that the idea of a basic income has grown in popularity. The Dutch city of Utrecht recently announced that it would be experimenting with a basic income in the summer of 2015. In the United States, a basic income has been advocated by policy analysts on both the Left and the Right.

A basic income would offer a social safety net—especially important in a time of economic instability. But it would also change the lives of its recipients in more qualitative ways. The basic income would ensure that individuals were financially solvent regardless of their jobs, decoupling economic status and employment. By offering money unconditionally, without a requirement for work or education, a basic income would offer financial support without stigma, unlike the current welfare-to-work system. Further, by giving individuals money that did not come directly from salaries, the basic income would also offer freedom and autonomy independent of waged work. Together with a shorter workweek, it would mean that individuals would be less dependent on their own labor to get by. It would give them room to explore their interests and ideas outside of work. It might very well give them more time.

Critics of basic income have argued that unconditional money transfers are no replacement for a strong welfare system, and indeed, a basic income cannot exist on its own. The sum given would have to be substantial yet not so large that it takes away from existing social welfare programs like health care and education. Further, while it would do much to reduce dependence on waged work, a basic income alone could not ensure that the burden of caregiving and household work would be distributed equally among men and women. Research done in Nordic countries suggests that gender-blind redistribution of money without incentives may not bring about equality between men and women; given the same amount of money to watch television as to nurse a child, an individual might choose the former. For this reason, the basic income could not be the only change; state supported childcare would be needed to take on part of the duties of housework.

So let us say that there is indeed a way to create more time. The question then becomes: Time for what? Weeks argues that it is only politically and socially acceptable to ask for time for two things: work and the family. Asking for anything else is considered extravagant, unrealistic, and worse—lazy. Yet life is not contained in these two spheres, and it neglects the wholeness of existence to try to shuttle it away into these two areas.

Thinking about a world with more time would entail a more theoretical shift: it would mean decentering waged work from a feminist conception of a better life. Since the second wave, much of feminism has upheld waged work and work outside the home as a way for women to find independence and freedom. Mainstream feminists have often praised the workplace as the site of great gains for women and encouraged women to work and better the conditions of their workplaces through activism, professional organizations, and legal campaigns. These efforts have improved the lives of many women by offering them economic stability and opportunities once only open to men.

But waged work is itself constricting and demanding—hardly liberation itself. As women have entered the workplace, the kinds of jobs they take have often declined in quality, paying less, demanding more, and becoming more unstable and restricting. Work does not foster independence or freedom when individuals cannot choose where they work or the conditions under which they do so. Placing work at the core of a feminist demand obscures work's problems and blinds us to life outside of it.

Instead, as we develop policies and steps forward, we should try to envision lives in which work is but one small part. What would people do with their free time? Anything they wanted! More time would mean better and stronger friendships, relationships not crammed in between work hours, family obligations, and sleep. It would give people the chance to explore their interests, creating room for activism or artistic endeavors. It would mean the opportunity for creativity and taking chances, but also fun and leisure and goofing off—all the things that are inaccessible when work consumes too much of the day. Most importantly, more time would mean not having to justify its use. One wouldn't need to *do* things with this time; one could spend it just by enjoying being alive.

Rather than fighting for more and better work, we should fight for more time to use as we please. Proposals like a universal basic income may well lead to this. Most importantly, in thinking about the time bind, we should keep in mind what it would mean to be really free from it. We should keep in mind the full possibilities of liberation: what we want is not to be allowed to work more or in better conditions, but to be allowed to live as we see fit.

Madeleine Schwartz *is a writer living in New York. She has written for* Dissent, *the* Believer, *and the* New Yorker's *culture blog.*

Imperfectly
A Feminist Utopian Economy that Embraces and Addresses Human Flaws

SHEILA BAPAT

A feminist utopian economy would possess two major characteristics. First, it would possess a fundamentally different definition of "family." Second, it would possess a robust public sector to regulate capital markets. Fundamental to both of these characteristics is truth: a feminist utopian economy would possess an honest understanding of the realities of both the private and public spheres and the flawed human beings that occupy these spheres.

Today we hold a romanticized view of what a family actually is: a team of people all moving toward the same goal. That view has long been mirrored back at us in popular culture—perhaps most obviously in shows like *The Cosby Show* and *The Brady Bunch*—which portray a sense of unity. The Bradys, after all, are a single bunch, as opposed to related individuals.

But a family is hardly a "unit." It is a gathering of distinct individuals who possess distinct desires and needs. For example, a working parent's desire to perform well at work is connected with her personal ambition, not necessarily its effect on her children.

A feminist utopian economy would appreciate this. It would understand a fundamentally different definition of what "family" really means. It would acknowledge the reality of diverging interests among family members depending on their role in the reproductive and productive realms. If *The Brady Bunch* epitomizes the current understanding of the cohesive unit, Louis C.K.'s show *Louie* gives us a taste of how citizens of utopia would conceive of family: following the eponymous character, his two difficult daughters, and his ex-wife, it correctly portrays a family as a collection of annoying people who all want their own way.

Following this baseline understanding, economic organization and policies would respond to individual family members' needs. Family members would retain some separate resources, rather than pooling all income, to ensure they can pursue their own dreams and interests regardless of their unit's approval—a change particularly important for women, whose freedom has historically depended on a father or partner's "allowance." The government will provide school tuition to ensure that a child's access to educational opportunities isn't dependent on parents' investment and priorities.

In addition, in a feminist utopian economy, the entire

concept of family would be pulled out of the "private sphere," a shroud (dependent on the idea of the unitary, conflict-free household) that disempowers women and children and dates back as far as modern history allows us to look. In *Democracy in America*, Alexis de Tocqueville approvingly observed that in the United States, "the inexorable opinion of the public carefully circumscribes woman within the narrow circle of domestic interests and duties and forbids her to step beyond it." As Catharine MacKinnon argues in *Toward a Feminist Theory of the State*, this lays the foundation for domestic violence being treated as a private "family" matter, one that should not be addressed by public resources such as police or public housing.

We should instead recognize that the front door of a home is not a magic wall behind which the rules and realities of public life have no relevance. Individuals build families within the context of broader communities, and what happens at home follows when they leave.

The utopian understanding of the public family would, by extension, mean the economy wouldn't distinguish between work in and out of the home—and so would be structured such that the labor of the domestic sphere is worthy of economic value. The understanding that care work is actually work rather than a quality inherent to mothers would be the norm, and the government would compensate both men and women for caring for their dependents. In building this utopian system, we'd be able to turn to American history for blueprints. Prior to welfare reform legislation of 1996, welfare was structured in a way that provided long periods of cash assistance to families. Family, in these cases, was defined as a pregnant or parenting woman and her dependents. However, welfare reform debates revealed that disdain for that system in part because the care work of single mothers was deemed *unproductive*. Welfare reform was designed to replace domestic labor with low wage jobs, necessitating that the children who would otherwise be cared for by their parent be placed in care of a patchwork of daycare, friends, and relatives.

But in a feminist utopian economy, welfare would be lauded for ensuring that all families in need have cash assistance because the labor of parenting is so important for healthy child development, and often so hard to manage while working outside of the home. The understanding that domestic labor is indeed real work is gaining more traction in our world today because of the domestic workers' movement—a movement to ensure basic labor protections for nannies, housekeepers, and caregivers—but this effort has not been without opposition.

How would this real work be compensated? A feminist utopian economy would not, necessarily, be an anticapitalist one. Instead, it might be regulated by a government that would acknowledge that greed and the quest for power are inevitable qualities in humans—and therefore must be controlled by a robust and fearless public sector and an equally robust and fearless feminist legal code that makes human rights its purpose above all else.

Critical to this robust public sector would be an acknowledgment of the value of all workers in the economy and stronger wages for all workers, along with protected and paid time off for illness or for the needs of family to ensure greed never overruns decent conditions for workers.

But why not imagine away all these human faults entirely rather than imagine how to regulate them? Acknowledging humans' tendency toward greed is critical to a vision for what is possible. A sanitized picture of utopia that erases the darker sides of human drive would be one in which we are never striving to be better. One of the key truths that feminist scholarship has conveyed is that feminism at its core challenges existing economic, political, sexual, religious, and other systems and how we've constructed them—about breaking them down and building up a new reality. It involves acknowledgment that humans are flawed, ever-changing, needing love, needing validation, and always moving in directions that earn them love and validation. A feminist utopian economy would not deny these realities, but embrace them.

Sheila Bapat *is a recovered attorney who now writes about gender and economic justice. Her first book,* Part of the Family: Nannies, Housekeepers, Caregivers and the Battle for Domestic Workers' Rights, *was released by Ig Publishing in 2014.*

Description of a Video File From the Year 2067 to be Donated to the Municipal Archives from the Youth Voices Speech Competition

DARA LIND
ILLUSTRATION BY RUTH TAM

A *high-school auditorium stage. The curtain is lowered behind a single podium, illuminated by a spotlight.*

A girl steps up to the podium. She's in the seventeen-year-old category for the competition, but she's short and slight. A few pieces of hair have already escaped her headband and fallen in front of her face; she tucks them behind her ear, clears her throat, and tucks her hair back again. She leans into the microphone. She repeats the name of her speech, as listed in the program, and on the name of the video file:

Do We Really Need Citizenship Ceremonies Anymore?

(She looks up at the audience, then, startled, looks back down at her index cards and tucks her hair back.)

When I think of citizenship, I think of my grandfather—my Aito. *(She blushes.)* Because being a citizen of the United States means more to Aito than to anyone else I know. He keeps a picture of all of us at his citizenship ceremony on the mantle, and he even has his tiny American flag framed next to it.

My Aito cares about a lot of things that most other people don't care about much anymore, like matching your pants to your belt, or dressing a baby in only pink or blue. My mother and I sometimes laugh at him for things like that, but we would never laugh at him for being proud of his citizenship ceremony. It just means so much to him.

But Aito is part of an older generation. And today *(she flips to a different note card, tucks her hair behind her ear again)* I would like to persuade you that in today's world, we do not need citizenship ceremonies. I will make the following points in support of my argument. One, that citizenship ceremonies used to be necessary but are out-of-date now because they're left over from laws that don't exist anymore. Two, that citizenship ceremonies are unnecessary because we welcome immigrants and value their contributions every day. And three, that citizenship ceremonies are becoming obsolete because private celebrations for new citizens, and for citizens who are just becoming eligible to vote, are already beginning to replace them.

(Flip; tuck.) When I started doing my research for this speech, I found out that citizenship ceremonies used to be called naturalization ceremonies, and at first I thought that was really weird. *(She looks out at the audience, and holds the look.)* Like people weren't naturally in America before they became citizens. *(She glances back*

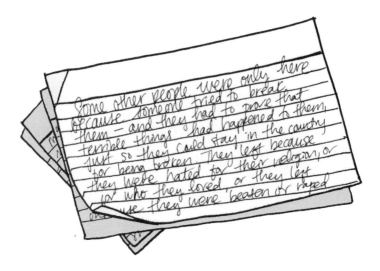

at the cards, frowns.) As I kept learning about the history, the name started to make sense. In the past, immigrants used to be cut up into all sorts of different groups. Different kinds of immigrants could only come here for certain reasons, and could only do certain things. That's the "papers" that everybody talks about in old movies. Some people were just here to be husbands, or wives, and couldn't work. Some could just work for one company or in one kind of job. It was like they were only parts of people. Some parts of their lives mattered, and some parts didn't.

Some people were only here because someone had tried to break them—and they had to prove that terrible things had happened to them, just so they could stay in this country after being broken. They left their homes because they were hated for their religion, or for who they loved, or they left because they were beaten or raped—and then they were required to make that the most important thing, the only thing, about themselves in order to come to America. And people who didn't have papers, it was like none of their lives mattered.

Becoming a citizen meant that you were officially a whole person again. That's what being naturalized was. So I think that, in those days, citizenship ceremonies were a good thing. They made it clear to everyone that these were whole people, not just parts to be used for one thing or another.

My Aito couldn't come because he didn't have the right parts. His sister, my Tia Abuela, came to the United States because her wife was here. But Aito was told he would have to wait for many, many years if he wanted to come along, because brothers weren't the right kind of family. So Aito stayed where he was and moved on with his life. He thought he had chosen between home and family for good. Even years later, when my mother came here, Aito thought it was too late for him, that he would never get the right parts to come.

My mother finally got Aito to come live here after my grandmother died. My mother needed help taking care of me because I was very small and got sick all the time, and she missed Aito. Aito could hardly believe he could come. My mother still teases him about it. *(She puts her hands on her hips, a little self-consciously, and pretends to look down, imitating her mother in a high voice.)* "I had to put you in a sack and put the sack in a suitcase and throw you in the luggage hold and keep you there, all the way to America!" *(A big laugh from the audience; she relaxes and flashes a smile before picking up her index cards again.)*

But I can't imagine what our lives would have been like if we lived fifty years ago, and Aito hadn't been able to come just to take care of us—because the government didn't think that being a caretaker for your family was an important enough reason to come to America.

My mom works, my brother and I go to school, and Aito keeps the whole household running. Aito makes me get up early if I want a hot breakfast—and extra early if I want to eat breakfast with my mom. He makes her hot breakfast before she goes to work at her firm—two eggs over-medium, even if she doesn't get up early. When I took my government class and told him that he was violating my equal rights by making my mom breakfast every day but not me, he stood with his arms crossed and made me tell him every amendment in the Bill of Rights—then he smiled, gave me a big hug, and made me breakfast in bed for a week because he was so proud of me.

And he's been just as much a part of our community as my mother, my brother, and me. His first month here, he marched right up to the city pool and signed up to give swimming lessons. He was so surprised that they didn't ask him for his papers, because he had heard from my Tia Abuela that she had been asked for her papers whenever she went to talk to a government official—to prove that she mattered.

On Sunday nights, Aito cooks a meal for all the kids in the neighborhood whose parents work late. He locks us all out of the kitchen. *(The audience laughs again.)*

Aito and Tia Abuela both still keep categories in their heads sometimes, about what parts of people count. They were very impressed when our next-door neighbors moved all the way from Nigeria to be doctors. They kept saying they were very skilled, because back when my Tia Abuela came to America, immigrants were more important if they were doctors than if they worked hard in the fields or cleaning houses—particularly cleaning houses, because that was seen as women's work. Now, I keep telling them that all people are skilled. Like that song says that we learned in kindergarten. *(She waits for a laugh of recognition from the audience, and doesn't get it. After a brief freeze, she tries to prompt them by singing it herself—self-consciously, only half-trying.)* "Ev-ry-bo-dy is a skiiiiilled body." *(A few laughs. Nervous smile.)*

I know why it's so confusing for them, because in the past there would have been a big difference between them and my neighbors. And even my neighbors wouldn't have been the same kind of immigrant. Mr. O would have come here to work, and Mrs. O would have come here to be his wife. She would have had to stay at home—and she hates staying at home. Every time I see her, she's out doing yard work, or going door-to-door in the neighborhood making house calls. Sometimes we don't even ask her to come over, but she hears my brother cough when he's playing outside, and she comes over with a stethoscope to check his chest. It's a little awkward, but it's because she cares so much about being a doctor—maybe even more than Mr. O does. She started working at her hospital the week they moved in here. I can't imagine her just being seen as Mr. O's wife.

And my mother! *(The exclamation is sudden, as if she just thought of this example.)* My mother didn't come here to be an architect. She didn't even know that was a thing that people did. She came here to be a gardener. She thought that if she came here to do a job, she couldn't stop doing that job to learn new skills—because that's how things used to be. She wouldn't have learned what architecture was because no one would have taught her it was something a girl could do, that was just how things were.

But when her bosses had their home renovated, she came extra early and left extra late to study the diagrams the surveyors and construction crews were using, and one of the surveyors told her that she could learn how to make those diagrams herself. She spent a week locked in her room working on her application to go back to school and get her degree. And the only difference for any of us was that she was home more often when we got home from school, while she was taking her classes, and then after she graduated and started working at her firm she was home less often again. We didn't have to worry about whether we would lose our right to be in America, or how we would get money for food.

(An apologetic half-shrug.) I don't even think about how it would have been different for my mother in the past. She's just my mother, and she did what she did, and anyone can do the same thing. So we don't need a "naturalization" ceremony anymore, to turn everyone into the same type of person.

(She pauses, then looks down at her cards. Her eyes widen and she frowns. Tuck. She shuffles a few cards. Double tuck. She closes her eyes, takes a breath, and looks back up at the audience.)

I would like to go back to what I was saying about skills to illustrate my second point: that citizenship ceremonies are unnecessary, because we welcome immigrants and acknowledge everything they do on a regular basis. One example of that, I think, is the way we tell people we don't know, "I appreciate your skills." When Aito and I went out when I was little, I heard strangers telling him that all the time. I learned that it was just good manners, like giving up your seat for someone on the bus. Now I say it when I see someone in a work uniform, or taking care of children or the elderly, or just when they look like they've had a long day. And the last day my mother worked as a gardener, her boss said it and gave her a hug—and then told her again, a few years later, right after she stepped off the stage at her graduation from architecture school.

Now that I know that skill used to mean a way to weed out certain people, that some immigrants had "skills" and some didn't, I understand that saying a lot better. People who worked in houses like my mother used to, or took care of children like Aito did—other people acted like they were invisible. A lot of those invisible people were immigrants, and a lot of them were women immigrants, and even though they were in people's homes and caring for their families, nobody thought that the work they did was important. I understand that the generation before us *(she looks directly at the judges' table, off to the right)* worked very hard to get to a society where people, and especially immigrants, are thanked every day for what they do. *(From a seat near where the video recorder has been set up, the audio track picks up a whisper, "Heh, suck-up.")*

But your generation already won! *(She freezes for a second, a little taken aback by her own vehemence. Then she sets her jaw, leans her elbow on the podium to get an easier view of the judges, and starts gesturing with her stack of index cards instead of reading them.)* We don't need to be defensive anymore. We don't need to say a few nice words to people when they become citizens, because we say a thousand kind and true words to them every day they're here. We don't need to try to persuade ourselves that we're the sort of country worth coming to. We already know.

(She starts addressing the audience directly again. Her hands are firmly on the sides of the podium.) This brings me to my third point. Citizenship ceremonies feel like they're not really about the new citizens themselves.

They seem like a way for everyone else to pat themselves on the back, for being worthy of everything they've given us.

And this is why—*(she flashes a triumphant grin and finds the final index card in her deck)* it's a good thing that private testimonial ceremonies caught on for new citizens. Ten years ago, approximately one in every twenty new citizens had a full private ceremony before the public one; now, a majority of new citizens have them. Attendees like these ceremonies because they want a chance to get up and talk about what the citizen has done for them, and to hear how she's changed others' lives. Before we hosted my Aito's ceremony, I hadn't known about the time he drove to my brother's school to take a classmate to the hospital when she broke her arm. And everything we ate at the block party afterward was cooked by my mother, my brother, and me. It was supposed to be a tribute to everything Aito has given us. But he wasn't happy when *he* was the one being locked out of the kitchen on a Sunday. *(A big, warm laugh from the audience.)*

People my age are beginning to hold testimonial ceremonies when we become old enough to vote—because in a way, we're new citizens too. When I reach voting age next year, I look forward to raising a glass of *(sidelong glance)* grape juice *(knowing laugh from the audience; big square-shouldered smile in return)* at my own testimonial ceremony. The America I see on those nights—that's the only America I've ever known.

(The audio track on the recording picks up a sniffle. The girl on-screen turns back to the judges' table.)

This is why I do not feel that we need public citizenship ceremonies anymore. Thank you.

The end of the file name is "3rd_Place_Speech." The last fifteen seconds of the file show the backs of a row of standing audience members, and the sound of a whole auditorium cheering and clapping.

Dara Lind *covers immigration and criminal justice for* Vox. *Previously, she worked in immigration advocacy. Her number one demand for utopia is commuting by jetpack.*

Ruth Tam *is a web producer at DC's NPR affiliate, WAMU. She has written and illustrated for the* Washington Post, PBS NewsHour, *and* Global Post. *She lives in Washington, DC, where she enjoys cheese, beer, and talking to strangers.*

Working Utopia

MELISSA GIRA GRANT

So I should say: I'm a very here-and-now kind of per-son and the way I talk about utopia in my work is gen-erally pretty tongue in cheek. When I am asked about anything in regards to feminism, it's most often about sex work. It's about feminism's sex work politics, which themselves are very rarely sex workers' own politics, but a feminism that uses sex work as an "issue," a litmus test, and not as a form of labor to investigate and orga-nize around, not as anyone's reality. Some feminists reduce sex workers to symbols of gender-based oppres-sion and violence, without regard for how sex workers experience oppression and violence—including from those who hold them up as symbols. There is little room for sex work in feminism's here and now, let alone its utopia.

So my cheek comes from being told too many times that a politics of sex work *here and now* is less important than to produce a sex work politics in order to advance feminism's utopian vision. The question "Is there sex work after the revolution?" is one you can debate without having to ask sex workers what they think. It's a debate without stakes. It's a fantasy.

But if you're going to go there and talk about a utopia without sex work, why stop there? Let's think about a utopia that includes no work, where there are other things people do to occupy their time, where people have other ways to fill their basic needs than deriving income by putting their labor to use for someone else. Let's think about disrupting what activity and value we put in the box called "work." Sex workers' utopias probably have much more to do with the rest of their lives outside of sex work. It's sex workers' politics that have shown me we reduce our lives to our work at our own peril. Very few people have utopian ideas about work per se. Most likely they'd rather there *not* be work. And that's not a particular indictment of sex work; that's an indictment of work itself.

I dug around for anyone who was talking about utopia in a way that made sense to me, and this is what Natalia Cecire has written, addressing tensions between queer generations facing oppression: "It is its own kind of shock to learn about how you have been historically rather than personally hated. It's not about trauma but about developing a political consciousness that is historical, a fundamentally utopian impulse to exist in solidarity with the dead."

So what I want, instead of outlining a specific feminist utopia, is a bolder feminist imaginary. I have all sorts of feminist imaginaries, some more personal than universal, even political. So yes, we must push beyond our current moment and imagine a better world. But most of the activism I have done, I know, is going to benefit people after I'm dead more than it's going to benefit me. Change just takes a long time. It's slow.

And when I think about the utopian responsibility of those who came before us, that's a way of confronting, with grace, the reality that it's the people who come one hundred years after us who live in this imaginary world we're striving for—that it's really about them, and what they imagine. In their utopia, I'm dead. I'm coming to terms with that. That's just how it's going to be.

As we imagine and reimagine our role in this future, we must get real about how fortunate we are to live in a moment where we are already well-prepared by those who came before us. Here and now, there is no shortage of smart theory and analysis and passion about sex workers' rights—we are the beneficiaries of more than forty years of international organizing by sex workers to make political demands.

So I think about what tools I can leave to others to take a new direction or to disagree with me. I don't want to shape a society so much as give others what they need to do it themselves.

That for me—leaving people the resources they need to realize the utopian vision of the future—comes out of harm reduction: people are experts in their own lives, you need to meet them where they are, and if you give them the resources they need to care for themselves, they will.

History is one of those resources. You have to know where you came from to have an understanding of both how unsingular you are and how not alone you are. Loneliness is a political killer. Isolation is a form of violence. Breaking isolation and breaking that feeling of no one having your back is so vital. And having fresh questions with which to walk into the future is a necessary resource. I am committed to taking questions about gender and sexuality and politics outside the realm of feminist debate and putting them back into the street and back into people's real lives.

It's easy to get caught up in designing politics for other people. Perhaps that's why feminists ask if there's sex work in a utopia—a desire for people to design a better society and ascribe some moral or rational process to how they decide who belongs there and who doesn't. But that's a genocidal road to walk down. The question that follows "Who belongs?" is "How will you extract the people who don't belong?" Historically and today, there has been no form of anti-sex work politics that doesn't also excuse the exclusion and removal of sex workers, that doesn't in some way justify violence against sex workers. That's why it's hard to even ask that question, "Is there sex work in our feminist utopia?" This is not neutral ground. This is a ground soaked in blood before we even got here.

Here's where I would invoke Silvia Federici, who wrote, evoking anti-fascist movements, "When you join such a struggle, you become part of something that projects you way beyond your own lifespan. The destruction of your own individual body means something different then. You build for the future."

Though I act as if it would have room for me, I accept that I won't be around for utopia. If a politics of exclusion doesn't ensure that, time passing guarantees it. So who will be here? Who are we building the future for?

Melissa Gira Grant *is a journalist and author. Her most recent book,* Playing the Whore: The Work of Sex Work, *challenges myths about selling sex and who perpetuates and profits from those myths. Her reporting and commentary has appeared in the* New York Times, *the* Nation, Glamour, *and the* Guardian.

Interview with Sovereign Syre

The following is excerpted from a conversation an editor had with adult performer and writer Sovereign Syre in Los Angeles on December 29, 2014.

If you could shift the adult entertainment industry so that it was as fulfilling for you as possible, what would it look like?

I think porn is really awesome and fulfilling, and one of the big paradoxes is that people say, "Oh, if you do porn, people treat you like you're shit." But the only people who've ever talked to me that way are *normal* people. That's *you* saying I'm worthless, that's *you* treating me that way.

What would happen if society at large didn't carry so much prejudice around the people who do porn? If no one villainized porn, how would the industry change?

It's impossible to say. I used to joke, "I hope porn never becomes accepted by society because I want to keep making money." There's a lot of money to be made in taboo.

But at the same time, maybe in an ideal world where there isn't the taboo, we could be compensated in better, more reliable, more just ways. Porn would be much more like mainstream Hollywood. You would have health care; you would get residuals. Right now in porn, you get paid for the work you do that day, but then those videos can be repackaged and resold and you never get compensated for that. And that's because porn isn't regulated the way Hollywood is because it's always been a kind of outlaw industry. So we don't have a union. You have SAG-AFTRA for mainstream stuff, but you don't have that for adult because it's so hard to talk about porn publicly.

There was also this book I read in college—I think it's called *The Managed Heart*—that primarily dealt with airline stewardesses and how emotional work is also work. I feel like porn is emotional work. Increasingly, porn is about selling intimacy. The majority of the work I get is requests for videos of me walking around with little to no makeup. Someone just requested a video of me listening to music and drinking tea.

It's emotional labor. And emotional labor is consistently devalued. But it's kind of the most important thing. In hospitals, where you have people that are sick, nurses and their bedside manner are as important to the healing process as actual procedures. Also, they did studies in the forties about the importance of touch in orphanages. A control group of babies was handled only during feeding and changing and the other group was held throughout the day. That second group had the healthiest development. So physical bonding and oxytocin are actually critical in our emotional and mental development—they are *necessary*. Porn stars, massage therapists, and airline stewardesses are all a part of that. Like you don't *need* stewardesses in a plane, but even on short flights, it calms people down. In a feminist utopia, then, all this work would be valued as important emotional labor that deserves respect and compensation.

What would happen if we viewed porn stars more like we view nurses?

If porn stars were viewed that way, you'd see a lot less porn stars with substance abuse problems. You'd see a lot more porn stars *enjoying* their work.

When I talk to my coworkers, the number one reason people quit has always been, "Oh, my boyfriend hates it," or, "My family is disowning me," or, "I can't have another job while I do this because my employer will find out." Consistently, the negative energy I've experienced in the industry has come from outside people having judgments about it.

For instance, people think they're giving me a compliment when they say, "You're really smart for a porn star," but in a feminist utopia that would be as weird as saying, "Oh, you're really smart for a lawyer," or "You're really smart for a nanny."

I'm more educated than 98.2 percent of the population. I have two degrees. I'm part of a very exclusive club. None of that matters because I am in adult films. Some guy living in his mom's basement feels like it's completely within his rights to question my intellect because I do sex work.

I lived with a legendary porn star for a while. And while we were living together she had a boyfriend. It was traumatizing to watch their relationship. He would constantly use her time in the sex industry against her. It was a way to easily win any argument. And she would internalize those judgments. And that's what I see happening all the time.

If porn was regarded as an important emotional labor or essential customer service people could enjoy the work without feeling shame or guilt about it.

You would never have to lie about what you do. I've been very fortunate to have a family that's incredibly supportive but I have to screen out other people who create static. In an ideal world, even super basic questions like, "Did you work today?" I could answer truthfully. I could say, "Oh, I'm doing a b/b/g [two boys, one girl] scene today, I've never done a boy–boy scene before so I'm super excited." I've been lucky to have friends that can be like, "Oh, that's really cool." And who can text me later and ask, "How did it go? Was it awesome?" Most people don't have relationships like that now. That's not common. Most people feel the need to hide. So you can't talk about your work. And you can't talk about *enjoying* your work.

If you're a doctor, you don't necessarily *want* to talk about your work all the time, but if you have especially satisfying moments on the job, you would never feel like you have to *hide* them. Your partner would never turn to you and say, "You're an awful human for enjoying yourself at work." As adults, people feel really comfortable saying those kinds of things because society says it's okay to shit on a sex worker.

A nanny is a caregiver. No one says to nannies, "Oh, you must actually *really hate* kids and you're only doing it to make money." In a feminist utopia, that kind of logic would also be ridiculous for people who work in porn. You could say, "I am actually really good at sex *and* I can make money off of it. For me, it's a really awesome job." But it doesn't even cross anyone's mind that I would choose this. They think women hate sex and assume if you're doing sex work or porn it's because you have to.

Social media has demystified a lot of these tropes already. On Twitter you can see that we're very much *people.* That we're not all damaged and in pain and in need of saving. Because you go on Twitter and you see girls tweeting constantly about loving their life.

In a feminist utopia, do you think sexual fantasies would change?

Absolutely. The trends that we're seeing now would continue as gender equality becomes more of a reality. I was just interviewing Dana Vespoli, who's a director, about the biggest change she's seen in the industry, and she said the variety. There are older performers, more diverse performers, more educated performers. There are more performers who are more politically aware and aware of how their images are affecting society. There's an increase in variety; there are sites where people can request custom clips.

And that's a reflection of gender equality because more of the people running those studios are women going, "I'm taking control of my own labor. I want to be the only one profiting from my emotional and sexual labor." So they become producers and creators of their own content. As women are taking control, we're figuring out that we can be smarter businesspeople and cater to exactly what people want. Before, all that people could watch was what big male-run porn studios dictated people should desire, and so that's all that viewers learned to desire. Now viewers can pay for custom experiences provided by savvy women who own their own labor.

So you're saying, as women take over the industry, it's like figuring out tailored medication, as opposed to older models of porn, where we kind of force-feed people one model of fantasy?

Yes. Consumers also now feel more comfortable asking for what they want. I think it's interesting that as that's happened, there's been a huge increase in the popularity of girl-girl movies and of the romance genre, which goes to show that, ultimately, what men and women want to see is actually female pleasure. And I think that's inspiring and good news. And full of hope.

The new taboo is fem-dom, because I think what a lot of men secretly want is to divest themselves of the role that society has given them. Men are constantly told this narrative that they have to enjoy plundering, conquering. And that is so harmful. When you actually start allowing men to ask for their own content, you see that they're *interested* in content with women feeling good. And they want to be released from the burden of being an ogre.

If we could openly value women's pleasure, if we no longer said that if you respect or desire a woman's approval, you're a pussy, we'd have fundamentally broken gender roles. And that's like Jenga. How do you pull that one out without the whole thing crumbling?

Embroidering Revolution

VERÓNICA BAYETTI FLORES

S urfaces wiped down.

Flowers arranged.

Dress pressed and ready to wear.

Altar dusted and set.

Lila walked back and forth across her apartment, inspecting and tidying every corner.

In a couple of hours, people from neighborhoods all over the city would be stopping in to see her works of art. She was a domestic artist, her works of art better suited for her home than a gallery. The home was the site of display and interaction and added essential context to the work. She had become known for her attention to every single detail, both in her intricate embroideries and textiles and in the environment in which they were presented. No color on the curtains was an accident, no plant on her windowsill lacking in meaning, no food served without thought—the rich histories of her kin and community woven into each element.

In the years since the Big Change, women and feminine-spectrum folks had ushered in a shift in the ways traditionally feminine art forms had been valued. Lila's abuela had been part of that revolution—part and parcel to the revolution of the Big Change itself, she had always said. Back when Lila's abuela was young, people didn't recognize her work as real art, mostly, as far as Lila could tell, because they were things that had been done traditionally by women and had been associated with the feminine. She had a hard time truly imagining it, but the detailed processes to which she dedicated herself so diligently—the painstaking stitching of her embroideries, the precise calculations, measuring, and cutting of her sewing—had instead been known as "crafts," kept distant from what was then called fine art. Keeping a beautiful home, making art out of textiles, and everyday cooking, were considered neat, maybe, but not really worth showing off.

Before the Big Change, people were only recognized for the ways they kept their homes or cooked if they were rich—if they used ingredients that were rare and cost a lot, or if they had a lot of things in their homes that were made by designers who would only create for those who had a lot of money.

But there weren't rich people anymore, or poor people, or money. After the Change, those who had relied on their riches to make things beautiful were left with the methods the rest of us had always used: our own hands and our own skills. Many of the people who had come from wealthy families were now learning techniques and skills passed down generation to generation from those whose families had never had wealth. Others just abandoned domestic creative pursuits altogether because they had only been interested in these arts as a way to show off. They had never engaged with the detailed and dedicated search for beauty in all things that Lila practiced.

For Lila's abuelita, the domestic arts had never been about ostentatious luxury. She, like Lila, had inherited a love for the small details and intoxicating beauty of domestic arts. Her folks, poor like many people were before the Change, had always needed to be resourceful. But they'd always made things beautiful, a practice where they could find unmitigated joy in a world that had so often been painful. The security that followed the Big Change was, for Lila's abuela and many others, an opportunity to expand, not abandon, her focus on the domestic arts that had always captivated her. And, of course, to pass them on.

It was Lila's abuelita who had taught her how to use onion peels, berries, beets, even black beans, as dyes, which she used to color yarns and fabrics and threads to knit colorful scarves, embroider family histories, or liven up an old dress. It was her abuelita who instilled in her the value of the work of the feminine, and Lila felt lucky every day for her abuela's part in building the world she now enjoyed. It was on days like today that Lila missed her most, when she wished her abuela could see the world she was continuing to build with so many others thanks to her legacy.

Just a couple hours left now.

Lila slipped into her dress. She applied the annatto lip color she'd made last week and blew a kiss to the picture of her abuelita on the altar. She could almost hear her say it: "*Suerte, nena.* You got this!"

Verónica Bayetti Flores *is a queer immigrant activist, writer, and artist. She has led national policy and organizing work on immigrant rights, reproductive health, and LGBTQ liberation.*

Equity Eats

EILEEN MCFARLAND

Hello, Equity Eats, can you please hold? Thank you!" I put the first caller on hold and then answer the second one. "Hi, this is Margaret at Equity Eats, please hold. Thank you!"

It's March 15, Ruth Bader Ginsburg's birthday and one of our busiest nights of the year for the Equity Eats restaurant chain. As is tradition, tonight every customer receives a complimentary fortune cookie with a quote from Justice Ginsburg inside. My favorite quotes are from the dissenting opinion she wrote for the 2014 *Hobby Lobby* decision, which, thank goodness, was overturned only a few years after it initially came down. One lucky diner will receive a fortune cookie that includes tickets to see a Broadway play with Justice Ginsburg. No one's opened the winning cookie yet, but we're at the height of the dinner rush and I know that someone will find it soon.

"Jamie, wanna switch so that I seat tables and you take calls?" The other managing hostess who's on the floor tonight gives me a relieved look.

"Thanks, M! You're the best."

"No sweat," I respond, and grab a handful of menus from zie. We just got another rush of customers in the door, and one family has a baby in a New York Liberty jersey who has already started to cry. "Shhh," I croon. "I know, honey, I cried when I saw our draft pick, too." The parents laugh, and the mom bounces her baby up and down on her hip in an attempt to make the little one stop crying.

"Do you need a space to feed your baby?" I ask.

"Oh, gosh, yes. That would be great," the mom says.

"You always have the option of feeding your baby at the dinner table while you wait for your food, or you could use one of the feeding rooms," I explain, referring to the space required under Restaurant Workers' Rights Bill No. 104a. "Do you think a diaper change is in order, too?"

The dad feels the baby's diaper, then scrunches up his face and nods yes.

I laugh. "No worries. Both of the feeding rooms have changing tables, and all of our bathrooms have changing tables, too. I can point you to the feeding rooms after I show you to your table."

"That would be great, thanks," they nod, and I lead them to their table in the Zora Neale Hurston room, after which I point them to the closest feeding room, right off the neighboring Nora Ephron room. The Nora Ephron room is one of my favorites, even if it can sometimes prove a memorable night when I seat families with young children there. Customers like to reenact the restaurant scene from *When Harry Met Sally* at the tables, and it can confuse the younger kids—although this isn't always a bad thing. One time, a daughter witnessed a reenactment and said to her moms, "Mommy, Mama, why is that woman having an asthma attack? Mommy, we need to help her! Give me my inhaler, now!" Then she ran over to the woman, almost tripping on her unlaced basketball high-top shoelaces, and offered the lady an inhaler. Her parents pulled up the kids' version of *Our Bodies, Ourselves* on the Kindle to explain that, no, the woman was just fine.

These days we're all feeling pretty good around here. Things have changed a lot since The Restaurant Workers' Rights Declaration. We're protected from sexual harassment, wage theft, and discrimination against workers with family care responsibilities. Plus, we're guaranteed not only benefits but also a higher base wage than workers received when they relied on tips.

I lead a few new diners to their table, and then come back to the hostess stand. My break is in twenty minutes, and you know that I'll be taking it with a nice, hot bowl of Equity Eats pasta. I should pick a dish high in iron, because my doctor warned me at my last appointment that my iron counts were low. All of Equity Eats' nutritional information is available if you ask for it, but nothing's plastered on the menu or advertised on the walls. I like it more than a place I worked at years ago, before the Declaration passed, where every two months they rolled out a new "Skinny Fusion" or "Reduced Guilt" this-and-that. At Equity Eats, we're not trying to fuse you into any new dress or make you feel less guilt about eating. We want you to feel full and we want you to know what you're eating. That's all.

Once my final twenty minutes are up, I go into the staff break room and kick off my shoes. Don't get me wrong: I love our restaurant-provided shoes because they have the perfect padding and grips to keep you comfortable for a long shift. Getting a podiatrist on board to design restaurant workers' shoes really was a stroke of genius from the Department of Labor. But, damn, it feels good to take off my shoes and put up my feet while I eat on break. After looking for the pasta dish with the most iron, I order up a plate of spinach fusilli with chickpeas, and Chef slides me a fresh batch with garlic bread and a fortune cookie on the side. Nice.

Jamie and Ayana get their breaks at the same time, so we all sit together at the big table and shoot the shit while we eat. Chef can hear from the kitchen, too, so sometimes he throws in a quip or two. We eat with appreciation and mindfulness. I can feel every bite of the garlic bread melting in my mouth, and it is perfect. "Chef, you did good!" I yell. Jamie agrees, then excuses zirself to go check on zir two kids in the restaurant-provided day care.

Finally, the fortune cookie. The paper my quote is written on has a heavier, stiffer feel than what Jamie and Ayana found. Ayana and I get quiet as I unfold the paper, and then we see it...

Broadway tickets for a show with Ruth Bader Ginsburg. If this isn't utopia, then I don't know what is.

A DMV native who currently stays in Chicago, **Eileen McFarland** *is proud to spend her days working toward health care for all. When she isn't enrolling clients in health coverage, Eileen studies coding at Blue 1647 and blogs.*

Interview with Miss Major Griffin-Gracy

SUZANNA BOBADILLA

The following is excerpted from an interview Suzanna Bobadilla conducted with Miss Major Griffin-Gracy in person in September 2014. Bobadilla is a writer, activist, and digital strategist based in San Francisco. For the past forty years, Miss Major, a transgender woman of color, has mobilized, supported, and led her community. She participated in the Stonewall Riots in 1969 and was politicized at the Attica prison in New York in the seventies. Today, she leads the Transgender Variant Intersex Justice Project. Through her current activism, Miss Major uses her experience in prison to shed light on injustices throughout the prison industrial complex and helps those who are still incarcerated and those who were released thrive outside the system.

To get things started, could you please describe what the word "utopia" means to you?

To me, utopia means the perfect existence in the most enjoyable space, with the most agreeable people, and a cohesiveness that builds toward individual and common goals.

Let's discover your feminist utopia through a day-in-the-life thought experiment. Imagine that it's the morning and you wake up to see that your utopia has arrived. As a self-described "glamour puss," you get dressed for your day. What are self-expression and performance like in your utopia?

Self-expression for me now is already what my utopia would be, simply because I don't give in to the dictates of this society.

As a transgender woman, I'm not always painted all the time. I'm not be-nailed and be-jeweled. [*Laughs*] It's how I feel that morning. If I feel like being bald, I look good! In my utopia, it would be important for me to be accepted for who I am in my guise. You don't need to put this mask on as if you are going out of your door to perform. You're just going out to take care of your business. Enjoy your day! Appreciate the people and things that are around you, and who appreciate you.

You hear these things like "you should paint" or "you should wear this," but that's not for somebody else to dictate. You should be able to choose what you like.

I strive to do that even now, and just accept the flack that comes with it. But if it was Utopia Day, there would be no comments about my performance, whether it was apropos or not, fitting or not. If it's one of those days where you feel like dressing cheap and in a short skirt, fishnets, heels, and pink hair—Go girl! Enjoy!

Brilliant! Continuing with our Utopia Day, you've now stepped out of your home and are walking through your community. You've strolled, said hi to folks, and you now arrive at work. What kind of work are you doing and who is joining you?

If this is utopia, I would hope that the work that you are doing benefits the society that you're living in and are a part of. What you are doing benefits others. You're doing something that you do best and someone else is doing something that they do best.

There is a human barter system going on. The needs of all are met by the skills of all. It isn't a thing of, "Well, I have more money than you." That doesn't matter in my utopia. It's a matter of, "I need this and so-and-so has it. Great, I'll go get it." If there is something that they need, I might have it or direct them to someone who has it.

Today, folks say that they want peace, but they don't do the things to have the peace. They don't do the things to work together. For example, there are so many agencies that are jumping on the transgender bandwagon because, "Oh, this is the flavor of the month. We have Laverne Cox, oh yay!" But what about the girls who suffered and died before there was a Laverne Cox? What about the girls who had to learn how to run in heels, keep their wig on, change their clothes, leap over cars to avoid the police, and become another person four blocks down the road? That's a skill! You don't just learn this! Practice makes perfect!

There needs to be some appreciation of those skills and prior activism, and in this "real world" we don't get that. I would hope that in utopia it would be acknowledged.

In your utopia, what would work look like?

In utopia, women would be getting paid exactly what men earn for doing the same damn job. My aunts and them worked so hard doing a job that men were doing, but they weren't getting nearly enough money to survive, take care of their family, and feed their kids. Everyone says, "Well, that's just how it is. That's the way of the world."

No, it doesn't have to be! It would be nice if this utopia would burst through and make itself known so that this kind of thing could stop. People appreciate that a woman gets so many months off after a baby is born. Well, give the dad so many months after his child is born. We should work on making this equal for one and all, not just for that person in the left corner in the red shirt!

Don't go erasing women who want to strip or be Playboy Bunnies. Encourage them for what they are doing. Have them do it safely. Make sure that they are not rid-ing around with some lunatic who is going to beat them to death because he has a problem. There needs to be a way for people to engage in the things that they choose and in a manner that keeps them safe.

Moving beyond work now, how are your friends and loved ones doing in your utopia?

In utopia, we'd have a compound and we'd be boogying down! The Kennedys can't be the only ones that have one! Miss Major should have one too, on a beach somewhere. Everyone would be dancing. Not that we play golf or anything, but hey, you can golf there, too.

What is friendship like in your utopia?

It's sincere and it's true. Your faults are accepted because nobody is perfect. Your friends don't try to change you into what they feel you should be to suit their needs. People rely on and trust one another and know what each other needs.

It's like having a husband or a partner or something, someone who will work with you toward mutual goals. You're not just supporting his work, his goals. He's not the president while you're the woman in the back doing dishes. Fuck that shit! Y'all should be doing this together! If he has a little office, give her a little office to let her do her separate, important, and divided thing. Period.

If you have a friend, you have someone to encourage you and to help you through the rough times. Things aren't always going to be easy, even in utopia. You're going to have moments of doubt, fear, or trepidation. Well, you need a sounding board, someone who you can trust and talk to, and who will give you their honest opinion. Not someone who is going to blow smoke up your ass.

What is love in your utopia?

It's all the things it should be. It's challenging, romantic, good, bad. You should get hazard pay! The hardest thing about loving somebody is when their faults start popping up.

It's like one of those old songs from when I was growing up, "Love is funny and it's not. It's bad and it's not." That's so true. I think the roller-coaster ride of it in a utopia would just be a little smoother than it is in the world that exists now.

This is a big question. How are transgender folks doing in your utopia?

In utopia, I would love to sit up and stand on my own two feet. This society is so hard pressed to let us get there. In utopia, for me, for the girls, and for the fellas, we would just blend in and be a part of society. Our work would be appreciated for the job that we could do, not who we are.

Guys won't ask transgender women, "How big is your dick?" What does that have to do with anything? Who am I as a person? Why are you talking to me? What is it about me that appeals to you? These men don't have time for any of that. They want to get into the perverse stuff. They want to get into the erotic "she-male" shit. A lot of us aren't "she-male." We are women who want to express ourselves.

Appreciating trans people's talents, skills, and passions would make it better for everyone! Nobody would have to prove anything; there wouldn't be any more bullying for young children who know well in advance of anybody else how they feel inside. That knowledge would be appreciated and nurtured. It's like plants! You give them food and sun and watch it grow! You don't throw bleach or piss on the damn thing or put it in the dark under a shelf.

If there was a utopia, it would be a blessed, growing, and nurturing place for everyone, not just my trans girls. Everyone would get a chance to exhale, to breathe.

And our final question for today: If I had asked you what your utopia would have looked like back in the sixties or seventies, would that answer be different from what you have given me today?

In the sixties as a younger person, it would be different simply because in your youth you can afford to believe in a utopia. Reality has not yet set in. You don't yet realize how cruel, devastating, and harmful the world and people can be. At that time for me, utopia would have been, "My group does my thing; your group does your thing." It would be separate.

Only through living through the real world do you realize that separate doesn't necessarily make it better. It's only better if it is inclusive. In doing social justice work, you try to get people to realize what's going on for humanity, not just for three percent of people.

In your youth, you don't realize that the clichés that you hear turn out to be so damn true. It's mind-boggling for me to see that. Now that I read those children's Dr. Seuss books, all of those things have some substance that would create a utopia if people allowed children to believe instead of saying, "It's just a fairy tale, that's simply not true."

The utopia won't exist because you won't let it. But if you let it, how wonderful would that be? I always remind adults of the story about the Sneetches with stars. The Sneetches first show prejudice to those who don't have stars but then to those who do! They eventually create a machine that makes stars, but then removes stars! It was pandemonium! Eventually, the Sneetches realize that stars, no stars, they are all fine! How wonderful that is!

Everyone does not need to be the same. What's wrong with accepting people for their differences instead of seeking them out and picking on them?

An Unremarkable Bar on an Unremarkable Night

s.e. smith

Three friends drift down the street and enter a building to attend the weekly anarchofeminist book club, where they peruse early twenty-first-century texts and imagine what life was like then. When all the speeches are over and everyone's milling around in the lobby, talking about the thought-provoking material discussed, the friends run into some acquaintances. The group decides to go out to a restaurant to have some tapas and drinks and continue their conversation. At the end of the night, they thank each other for a great time before making their separate ways home and promising to meet up again soon. It's an entirely unremarkable evening.

In this utopia, it is unremarkable that all the people at the event experience equal pay for equal work, fair treatment, and a world without racism, homophobia, economic disparity, religious intolerance, transphobia, classism, and fat hatred. Of course they do. These are things that are taken for granted in utopia. Though their ghosts live on in horror novels and the weekly book club reminds them how bad people once had it, they're abstract things.

This evening is also unremarkable because, in this future where our friends live, Friends A and C didn't have to think, or worry, about access issues at any point. Friend A knew that the sidewalks would be wide and clean so she could move down them comfortably in her power chair without being forced into the street or having to jump curbs. She knew the event would be held in a fully accessible building with a ramped front door and accessible bathroom. No one would gawk or stare at her, although she uses a respirator to help her breathe and a communication board to chat with her friends. She knew that they wouldn't have to check ahead to determine if the restaurant was accessible, and that they wouldn't arrive only to discover that despite a promise that it was, there was "just one step" or the bathroom doors were too narrow for her to enter. No one would point or laugh at her because she was trans; instead they would welcome her into society as the woman she is. Her transition had gone smoothly for her. She'd been respected throughout the process, which included the transition services she needed, fully funded through the government's single-payer health-care plan.

Friend C knew that her service dog wouldn't be distracted by people trying to interact with him, and that all the materials at the event would be presented in audio as well as visual form. And she knew her friends would seamlessly integrate descriptions of the visuals around them into their conversation when these things were relevant. When the menus were passed around she would know which dishes were gluten-free. She knew that the restaurant staff would take her gluten sensitivity seriously, and would consider any possible areas for cross-contamination in the kitchen.

Meanwhile, Friend B breast-fed and dandled her infant on her knee openly and comfortably, knowing that the restaurant would accommodate her. The three were seated in a quiet, comfortable area where it would be easy to sit and talk, and where the baby would be least likely to be disturbed. No one asks Friend B who the father is, or where he is, or why the baby doesn't look much like her. No one would ask why it is that a black woman has a light-skinned baby.

This is a society of free and open accommodation for difference, where a thousand tiny gestures of acceptance and welcome have replaced the thousand tiny cuts that women had to endure before utopia. Our three friends live in a world of complete and open access, of inclusion, not simply tolerance. They are woven into the very fabric of society with a quiet, deft skill as part of the amazing and astounding spectrum of humanity, respected as individual people with tremendous contributions to utopia's past, present, and future.

Their disabled forbearers were there at the incipient

beginnings, when labor organizers fought in the early twentieth century to get children out of factories and cut down on working hours.

They knew, as perhaps no other fighters for utopia quite realized, that disability directly affects some 20 percent of the population, and touches many more. It is part of the fabric of everyone's lives. Anyone can become disabled at any time: a car accident, a sudden illness, the gradual decline of age. In utopia, disability is as much a part of society as breathing (with a respirator or otherwise), and one would as soon open an inaccessible business or make a rude comment to a disabled person as one would sexually harass a coworker. Our friends live in a utopia where the approach to disability is not one of dehumanization, fear, and eliminationism, but of welcome. "Oh, you're deaf?" signs a conference organizer for an academic event on twenty-first-century feminist protest chants, "Our staff interpreters are right over there!" They live in a utopia where disabled people are welcomed into feminist spaces and celebrated as a vital part of the community, where feminism honestly confronts its troubled relationship with disability and, through hard self-examination, has embraced a politics of radical inclusion.

When she was born, Friend A's parents had the full support of their community and a well-paid, well-trained home health assistant funded by the government to help Friend A live independently—and no one had ever suggested they abort her when they got the diagnosis. Friend A's parents never lacked for support and respite care as Friend A grew up. At no point did anyone assume that they should be her primary, unpaid caregivers. Her parents received state assistance for equipment, creating an accessible home, and accessing professional aides for daily living and support in school. When she moved into her own apartment, an ample government grant helped her while she got settled and found work doing what she loves: mapmaking and sociological cartography, using maps to study trends over time and place.

Friend C is thinking about having kids of her own in a few years with her girlfriend, and the two have talked about which one of them will carry the baby. Friend B teases them over their fierce competition. They aren't afraid of losing their children, not in utopia, where county clerks use ungendered forms for birth certificates, with room for two, three, or even more parents, and where the parenting abilities of disabled people are never challenged on prima facie grounds. Throughout her life, Friend C has been surrounded by people who believe in her. No one has told her she can't be a mother because she's blind, and she, like other disabled parents, can access mentoring and parenting classes specifically geared toward her impairments.

Utopia isn't senseless to difference, but it embraces and warmly welcomes it rather than fearing it. Indeed, utopia is a rather unremarkable place. It has become the shared reality of a million dreamers, the lived experience of generations following from those who fought long and hard for it. Utopia is not something taken for granted—it is warmly and ferociously protected—but it is also the mainstream. It is a dream accomplished not solely through endless legislation, though laws played a key role in realizing utopia, but a dream achieved through the everyday work of millions of ordinary people, all over the world.

Friend A keeps two photographs on her wall: One, the famous image of ADAPT protesters crawling up the steps of Congress, fighting for the Americans with Disabilities Act, a reminder of the indignities and suffering people endured as they struggled for self-determination in a world that largely ignored them. The other, from a trip to London, Friend A grinning in her chair under the sculpture of a defiantly pregnant and disabled Alice Lapper in Trafalgar Square. It's a reminder of a pleasant holiday, but also of the immense controversy over the statue. When it was installed, Lapper's form had been deemed hideous and inappropriate. It offended the nondisabled establishment's ideas of beauty and parenthood in an era ruled by ableism and prejudice. These images are not just history, but a reminder of a bitter past, and a warning of an ominous future should those living in utopia forget it. Friend A remembers, because she never wants utopia to fade away.

s.e. smith *is a writer, editor, and agitator based in Northern California. smith enjoys challenging readers and writers alike to work outside their comfort zone and consider their own role in shaping a new world of possibility. You can find smith's work at sites like the* Daily Dot, xoJane, *and the* Guardian.

Lesbo Island

JILL SOLOWAY

My entire life has been leading up to this: a call for an unarmed yet mighty revolution, secession into an all-female state, with a big ol' newfounded land, sort of a gigantic, utopian honeycomb hideout, ruled by me, yes me, until the patriarchy is toppled and a matriarchy run by me, yes me, is installed. It's freaky: it doesn't matter if I start out writing about firemen or Tostitos or poodles, everything seems to drift back, like a shopping cart with a broken wheel, to the idea that the only solution to everything wrong with everything is to start a woman-ruled planet, and to begin by starting an all-woman land.

After I get the first couple of girls there, I probably shouldn't tell the rest of the converts that it's forever. This could scare a few women off, women who are probably dominated by their ingrained love of the patriarchy or addiction to blended drinks from the Coffee Bean and supermarket sushi. These are the women I would have to trick. To start, I'd just call it "my land," not "our land."

In fact, just to be safe, I wouldn't even call it Lesbo Island, nor Wombtown, I'd call it something lovely and lite, like Feather Crest, so people wouldn't have any idea what I was up to. They'd turn up for the nature walks or to sample my slow-roasted meats, or perhaps to find their muse walking by the pond. But once there, spending their long mornings and magical afternoons and oh-so-starry nights under my quiet, unspoken rule, they'd start to realize: now *this* is life. Long weekends would turn into just another day, until they'd been there a week, then a month.

Our first Feather Crest Village would be a mock-up for the rest of the lands that other women would make after ours goes really, really well. On about forty acres, we would situate eight or so small cabins, all hidden by enough woodsy goodness that no one could see into your house from their house. This way, any women who wish to do naked stretching can feel free. Nudity will not be encouraged in other parts of Feather Crest, however. No one should expect to turn up and strut around the pool with their bush on display. That's for inside your cabin.

Every cabin will have its own wood-burning fireplace and kitchen. Women are encouraged to purchase their own groceries and eat in their own homes as often as they wish. In the center of the land, however, would be the (ROUND!) center house—make that Centre Haus—with a giant industrial kitchen, a gathering room (ROUND!)

with a fireplace, a gigantic round plasma TV, plus the shed where you keep your blow-up rafts when you don't feel like deflating them for the fall.

At Feather Crest, we'd be the village some say it takes: I could be tap-tap-tapping on my computer while Lisa hangs out in the vegetable garden with everyone's kids pointing out the difference between arugula and frisée. Later that day, Sammy would gather the kids for finger painting while Lisa and I took the station wagon into town for supplies. Every few months, the men would come up for a few days, but as time passed, everyone's relationships would be ruined and instead of visits we'd get checks. If the checks weren't enough, we'd write books or sit in a circle and craft hammocks to sell on the Internet.

And it wouldn't have to be hammocks, it could be beaded bracelets or seashell paintings, anything where we sit in a circle and laugh, babies popping on and off of breasts to nurse, while through the screened-in porch, we'd watch the older children delight in faerie games. All of that stuff sounds so dang much better than the urban, over-scheduled playdate land I live in right now. I only see my women friends every couple months, when we plan a Girls' Night or Ladies' Sushi Night. That's right, we actually have to name it to make it happen.

On the land, nothing would be planned. *You only come to the Centre Haus if you want to.* No planned meals, no chore wheels, no meetings, no yoga. If you're at your cabin and you desire some company, you can walk to the

Centre Haus to see what's doing, but by no means can anyone write up a notice saying "Deb's Vegetarian Chili Nite at the Centre!"

Any sort of planned group gathering is a recipe for disaster. Nearly all of my daily problems here in the real world are rooted in disdain for plans already made. If I could remove commitments from my life, my mood would improve by at least 13 percent. All my friends seem to feel that way lately too. Most complaints start with, "I told Brett I would be at her birthday gathering, but I got my period." It's the same for my kid. Saturday mornings start with, "Do I really have to go to Mia's birthday party? Can't we just stay home and watch all those *Wife Swaps* that TiVo is about to erase?"

At Feather Crest, there are no planned gatherings, only spontaneous ones, so obviously, that rules out Evites, which I've been trying to find a way to do away with for a long, long time. All of the food would be constantly growing, fresh in the Gardenne outside of the Centre, so if there was a sudden rush of people needing to have, say, an unplanned eighties dance party, there'd be plenty of red chard outside that could be gathered into a basket and boiled into sustenance.

Also at Feather Crest, as I've implied, there'd be no men as permanent residents, with a few exceptions. Anyone's son who was raised there can stay there until he's twenty-five. Tradesmen from the local town could visit for our ever-lessening sexual needs. If the pool of contractors gets shallow, we might need some manner of Man Wheel on the fridge so no one steps on anyone else's conquests. Ex-husbands—but only those bringing checks—can stay for a long weekend (Thursday through Sunday or Saturday through Monday but *never* Thursday through Monday); plus any men I say because I'm Queen.

Speaking of which, this is the number one rule at Feather Crest, and hopefully, in the rest of the world once I'm Queen:

No killing. This is something men don't understand. They think one has to be able to kill to let eternity know man is here to stay and means it. Super Goddess, the entity to whom we'll pray out at Lesbo Island, knows that the taking of a life is a job for nature only, not man. This one seems really obvious to me, as obvious as lifting the toilet seat if you're going to hover, but there are millions and millions of men in uniform and in suits who still don't have this one figured out.

Killing is wrong. When I am Ruler of It All, negotiations between nations would start with that awareness, that no man is allowed to take another man's life, even as punishment. It's the ultimate sin against god, the gods, God, nature, whatever you want to call it, just don't do *that*. Okay?

Sure, maybe it's okay if you wanna do other stuff, sure, cheat on your husband or take the lord's name in vain, that's all negotiable. I personally love to take the lord's name in vain; I call out, "Jesus on a Cracker!" when I stub my toe. Do whatever the fuck you want, just *stop kill-*

ing people. That one seems so obvious to me. No killing. Except, if you get really old and annoying and kvetchy, we can kill you. I wonder if that will still be funny to me when I'm old. Probably not.

Also, no one can hurt anyone, unless you're Daphne Merkin and you're visiting and you provide written, informed consent to getting spanked.

If lesbians need to escape from their partners, I don't know which one will come to Feather Crest, but that's up to them. I only ask that if both sides of a lesbian couple come, they don't fight on the veranda.

This talk of lesbians makes me think of my sister Faith. She came out when she was in her early twenties. It was a surprise, yet, as soon as she told me, it put into order everything that had come before. When we would go to buy clothes, my sister would end up in tears. I can still see her looking in the three-sided mirror at Saks, turning this way and that in her gauzy floral dress with sleeves fashioned out of scarves. I don't know what she saw. It was something so incongruous it made her cry, although there were no words. Just the familiar feeling of, oh god, Faith can never find anything to wear and now we have to go home early, and I'm pissed because everything looked great on me and I can only buy one outfit.

But as I got older, I began to feel more like Faith when it came to dressing like a woman. From fourteen to twenty-one-ish I was happy to don the leggings and miniskirts proscribed by *Seventeen* magazine. After that,

I went into worker mode, as a personal assistant and documentary film person and then writer. I could wear jeans and funny vintage T-shirts and be just like a boy at work. But now that I'm a woman, it is expected that on certain occasions I put on a dress. And now, when I stand in the mirror, I feel less like a lady. I feel wrong. I want to cry.

Those pointy shoes make me want to cry. Anything Sarah Jessica Parker ever wore makes me want to cry. Dresses that wrap or are strapless or empire-waisted make me fall to the floor in a crumply pile. When Steve Madden shoes were in, I could pull off a heel for a while, finally getting some height, yet staying comfortable, up high on my thick Frankenstein chunky feet. But last year I was going to a meeting and looked down at my Steve Madden Mary Janes, the top part a brown-on-brown rendition of a schoolgirl shoe, all sitting atop a slightly curvy black brick they called a heel. It was just like the moment that came a few years previous when I looked down at my miniskirt and I said to myself, "This is the last day I'll ever wear a miniskirt." And I was right.

As I stared at my clunky Madden nineties clodhoppers, something else was clear. Previously I'd never understood how all those old women were still wearing those big bouffant hairdos that took an hour and a half to set, once a week at the beauty salon. But now I realized what was up. These women were still wearing whatever they were wearing at their primes. However their hair and makeup and clothes looked when they were nineteen, they stuck with. I'll stand, they said to the fashion world. No more cards. Because they felt confident for a brief stretch between postpuberty blush and the sags of age and because this was the moment when they got the most head-turns, they were holding onto it and not letting go, not for their lives, like the way my mom's dog acts when he finds one of her bras on the floor.

I saw myself at eighty: I'd be stomping over to my Adult Day Health Facility in my thick black-heeled clodhoppers, with a miniskirt and an ironic T-shirt and long, greasy, flat-ironed gray hair. I'd be like an elderly version of Bratz. Geriatz. That day when I got home I put all my thick-heeled shoes into a bag and threw them up into the hole in the ceiling to the attic. I knew one day I would go up there with my grandchildren, and we would laugh, yes, how we would laugh.

If all of this is sounding good to you right now, tell your girlfriends, no pointy shoes or strappy stilettos, no pantyhose, no waistbands. I'm not saying it's a place to get all sweaty and wear muumuus. I do believe bras will still be appreciated; I want everyone to be comfy. But at Feather Crest, we'll get to the business of our lives first and the constriction of appearing womanly somewhere far, far down the list.

Oh god. Here I am again. It's not that I hate men. I really don't. I'm just mad that I have to walk into bookstores and find a tiny section called Women's Studies. Why can't the men have the tiny section? Why can't most of the books, the books about being human, be written by women? I want to be the syllable (man); I want *them* to be the amended syllable (wo-man).

I believe I know the reason we have to start Feather Crest, if my plans for the matriarchal overthrow are ever going to take off. It's possible the reason is hidden in the text of *The Da Vinci Code*, if only I had the patience to read it. I think it says something like Mary told Jesus everything he knew, and that sounds about right. Yes, it is time for the change, the end of the way it has been. Time for the righting of the original wrong that was done way back when man first noticed woman was powerful, and as antidote to their powerlessness, men went and built everything, every single thing that I have to fucking live under, including, but not limited to, a God they call He, Jesus, Allah, and *Maxim* magazine.

So, sisters, give me time. Keep an eye out for the ads, though they may be a few decades down the road.

Maybe people will start to take notice of Lesbo Island—I mean, Feather Crest—and it will bring back that resurgence of feminism I keep calling for. Are we really done with making noise?

No! We will shout from the tops of our roofs at Feather Crest, if we can find the ladders.

No, at Feather Crest you will let your hair go free and your bushes go wild. We offer no enforced blow jobs, childcare, or cable. Of course, you need to buy this book, so if you're reading a friend's copy right now, get your own because you'll need it when you apply. You should also probably think this essay is great, super great in fact, for it will be our manifesto, actually, our woman-ifesto, not to be confused with Cuntifesto, a festival we have twice a year with really good barbecue.

Jill Soloway *is the creator of Amazon Studios's* Transparent, *which won a Golden Globe in 2015. Jill won the US Dramatic Directing Award at the 2013 Sundance Film Festival for her first feature,* Afternoon Delight. *She is a seven-time Emmy nominee, the author of the memoir* Tiny Ladies in Shiny Pants, *and the cofounder of Wifey.tv, a video network for women.*

Noisy Utopia

KARLA SCHICKELE

Every summer I get a glimpse of a kind of feminist utopia. It's not an actual utopia because it's real and it's flawed, but it works—and it's joyous and noisy, slightly magical, and really fun.

It's a rock camp for girls. I've gotten to see it every summer for ten years now. Technically, it's a one-week camp where girls and trans youth create music collaboratively and ask questions of the world, with the encouragement and support of adult mentors. But for me, rock camp has also always served as a powerful window into what's possible. It feels like a one-week snapshot of what a community can be—what our utopia could be—if it's grounded in feminist values. Imagine an issue of a mainstream music magazine that covers the sonic experiments, lyrics, and artistic choices of various female artists—but it's not the "Women in Rock" issue, it just happens to be that all the artists of note that month are female. Imagine a world in which "girl bands" are just *bands*.

When I walk around rock camp, I hear sixteen bands made up of girls playing music they created together by taking chances and listening to each other's ideas. They're playing unapologetically and on their own terms. The music defies genre. I'm struck by the range of topics and voices and ideas.

There's plenty of humor at rock camp. Kindness is considered the norm, not a feminine trait. There's a wonderful absence of snarkiness. That particular kind of mean-spirited, competitive energy that's rooted in self-doubt and fear is largely missing, too. In the main space, where our full community gathers several times a day, there's a wall covered with "shout-outs," which are cards and post-it notes—"Fiona, you rock," "Nia, I love being in a band with you!" They are casually posted on a wall for all to see. They are not displayed under duress, like pieces of flair (my favorite dystopia is without a doubt the world portrayed in the movie *Office Space*). They are testaments created and shared because it's in the air of the place to do that kind of thing, without irony or embarrassment.

Where could this spirit be found in a feminist utopia? Maybe it would be high schoolers posting to a "put up" (instead of a "put down") message board after a talent show to offer shout-outs to everyone who had the nerve to get up on that stage. What if it was considered cool to express support for other people even if they're not your friends?

At rock camp, youth and adults tend to listen to each other, and when possible, they solve problems together. We make group agreements at the start of the week to be safe and respectful; they are not a magic wand, but when we do need to check in with the commitments, knowing that they were generated by all the people in the space makes it feel strikingly different from the exercise of enforcing rules.

What if these kinds of agreements ruled the world? What if schools started each year by gathering the school community—students, teachers, staff, parents, and caregivers—to create agreements together? Necessary rules for safety and health could be included in that process, with a chance to discuss *why* they're needed (a move that greatly increases chances of people following them). And there would be room for everyone's ideas about how to show respect for one another, and what to do when group agreements aren't honored.

Places like rock camp help us dream, while we also create and put into practice the values that many of us would like to see reflected more often in the world.

What if you were at rock camp, too? You might love it. And if you did love it, and we all loved it, what if we just kept doing it? What if we started making our parallel universes one week at a time, and then expanded all of those weeks until they touched, and extended them over time, and they became just the way things are?

I'm in. How about you? Let's start a band.

Karla Schickele *is a musician and songwriter and the founding executive director of the Willie Mae Rock Camp for Girls in New York City. She lives in Brooklyn with her partner and their sons.*

Finding an Erotic Transcendence
Sex in a Feminist Utopia

LORI ADELMAN

In touch with the erotic, I become less willing
to accept powerlessness.

—Audre Lorde

For almost as long as the movement has existed, feminists have been painted as prudish and sex-negative. Early suffragettes were dismissed as "lonely frigid women who crave attention" by Herbert Asquith, Prime Minister of the United Kingdom at the time. In the once-popular 1959 book *The Power of Sexual Surrender,* Marie Nyswander Robinson attributes to feminists "a frigidity and restlessness." In two more recent examples, ABC News described *feminism* as "a sexual buzz kill— a veritable *anti-Viagra*," and Andrea Tantaros suggested on Fox News that "after years of bra-burning" feminists are likely to wake up one day and find themselves old, unmarried, and "not getting you-know-what."

It is not only the movement's opponents who contribute to this characterization. I was one year old when Andrea Dworkin published her now infamous *Intercourse*, and it would be years before the term concerned me at all beyond having been recently conceived by the method. To be fair to the much-maligned author, Dworkin never went so far as to state that all heterosexual sex is rape, though the statement is often misattributed to her (she has confirmed in subsequent interviews that this was never her belief). In fact, *Intercourse* contains an underappreciated eroticism and complexity, as in: "Sometimes, the skin comes off in sex. The people merge, skinless. The body loses its boundaries. We are each in these separate bodies; and then, with someone and not with someone else."

Yet despite such elegant forays, the book paints heterosexual sex as fundamentally concerned with and distorted by patriarchy. Thus, Dworkin's text has (fairly, I think) come to represent a school of feminist thought in which sex, or at least the heterosexual kind, couldn't really be "good" or "feminist" so long as misogyny was present in society.

This is a distinctly dystopian view, and one that hasn't held up over time. Sex-positive feminism, derived in almost direct opposition to this Dworkinian line of thinking, is much more the *mode du jour* (though truthfully it's grown enough to face its own backlash and spinoffs in recent years). As *Intercourse* and I near our mutual thirtieth anniversary, I've come to count myself among the many feminists currently living in our decidedly imperfect world who happen to love sex very, very much. Others who seem to be hanging out in this club with me include: Dr. Ruth, Beyoncé, Sady Doyle, Tristan Taormino, at least a few of the dancing-alone-to-Pony people, and maybe even your parents.

This all to say: for many people, sex is already a pretty great—and feminist—endeavor. And for many feminists, improving the conditions of humankind's sexuality is central to their efforts.

Still, these efforts are majorly hindered by good old misogyny, and all the sexually ruinous baggage it brings. With the elimination of misogyny and the rise of a feminist utopia would come a number of breakthroughs to drastically improve the sexual experience for all. In particular, there are three core barriers to pleasurable sexuality—all of them tied up in antifeminism—that would be solved in a feminist utopia. The first is cultural stigma and shame around sex and pleasure, especially when associated with womanhood and femininity. The second is restrictive, retrograde gender norms. The third is the laws and policies around reproductive health care and information.

Stigma

Stigma and shame around sex and sexuality are pernicious. Sometimes, as in the case of honor killings, they cost lives. Even in less extreme circumstances, they erode our understanding and acceptance of our own bodies and sexualities, and those of our partners. But this stigma is not distributed equally. Women, especially queer and trans women, too often draw the bulk of society's ire. There are many ways of naming this problem. Modern feminists rail against "slut shaming," calling out the double standard inherent to the "he's a stud, she's a slut" mentality. Audre Lorde writes that the erotic "has often been misnamed by men and used against women." Chris Kraus speaks of the deep "pity and horror" with which society treats female sexual desire. Even our most brilliant poets are guilty of treating sex as a "taking" of something from one person to another, a zero sum exchange of power.

In a feminist utopia, such taboos, regardless of what you call them, would not exist, let alone prevail. As individuals with autonomy, we'd determine how much sex we wanted to have, and face no negative social consequences for that determination, regardless of our gender identity or sexual orientation. Rather than hurling euphemisms for "loose" women at each other, we'd spend our days riffing on new dental dam flavors or debating feminist-identified porn stars. Teenage girls (or full-grown adult women, for that matter) wouldn't be bullied for being "whores," "sluts," and "fast-tailed girls" or face obnoxious double standards. Instead, they would coin new nicknames ("Charlottes"? "Sirens"?) to celebrate and honor their own agency in seeking pleasurable sexual experiences. Upon hearing of a happily sexually active lady, we'd praise her pleasure and ask for tips. First female orgasm would be a milestone on par with first menses. And monogamous, heterosexual relationships would no longer be a precondition for acceptability, but rather two variations of a virtually never-ending set of circumstances under which female sexuality—or any sexuality, for that matter—would be socially acceptable. No longer would we feel pressure to bring a marriage-track boyfriend to grandma's birthday bash. In fact, we could comfortably go alone, or bring our two partners, or bring the person we slept with last night, without facing stigma or judgment from our family or friends.

Gender Norms

Beyond stigma, modern sexual life is fraught with gendered expectations, roles, scripts, and concerns. These impede erotic intimacy at the most fundamental level by making it more difficult for us to be true to ourselves, and to trust our lovers to accept us for doing so. They also have negative implications outside of the erotic realm. Though we're already seeing an upswing in public support for progressive ideas about gender, parents are still more likely to abuse gender nonconforming children, for example, and the media is more likely to then blame them for their own abuse.

In a feminist utopia, such roles would be disempowered. Depictions of beauty and sex in media, from fashion magazines to pornography, would represent a wide range of aesthetics, preferences, and experiences, seamlessly incorporating queer and straight sexualities with trans, cis, intersex, and gender nonconforming bodies. In a feminist utopia, we could ditch the uncompromising scripts in favor of liberation through gender self-determination, and all people would have the opportunity to establish and define what "good sex" really means for ourselves and our partners. "Honey, should I wear that thing we like tonight?" would frequently be uttered by a person of any gender, in reference to anything from high heels to lipstick to strap-ons. Sex would be considered as a form of creative personal expression, similar to painting or drawing, so it would be ridiculous for someone else to attempt to impose their own rules and standards.

Laws, Policies, and Education

From antisodomy laws to abstinence-only education initiatives to parental consent laws, sex and reproduction are highly politicized and heavily regulated, often to bigoted and discriminatory effect. Although we often experience sex very personally, in order to pursue and protect our collective human right to pleasure and positive sexual experiences, we must engage with it on the political level. In a feminist utopia, sex-positive laws and recognition and enforcement of sexual pleasure as a human right would be the law of the land.

It's difficult to envision how this would actually work, but one can uncover hints of this model in a document published by the International Planned Parenthood Federation. In *Sexual Rights: an IPPF declaration*, ten articles are outlined, each grounded in and informed by actual international agreements such as United Nations conventions and treaties. Included among these are the right to security and bodily integrity, the right to privacy, the right to personal autonomy, the right to health and to the benefits of scientific progress, the right to education and information, the right to choose whether or not to marry and to decide whether or not, how, and when to have children, and the right to accountability and redress.

In a feminist utopia, such rights would be assured by law. Policies would be in place to bolster sexual health and access to reproductive health care, not limit it. Abortion would be available on demand, in state-of-the-art compound facilities decked out with flat screen TVs, vintage shopping boutiques, and delicious restaurants; the doctors and nurses on staff would be well paid, polite, and medically gifted. Sex workers would be guaranteed safe working conditions by law and would be bolstered by social norms that would consider stiffing or harming a sex worker to be an unacceptable offense. Service providers who object to reproductive health-care access would be out of a job. Racial disparities in health-care access would be unconstitutional. The time of legal restrictions and barriers to access would be over, and the era of proactive sexual and reproductive health policies would reign. And rather than be kept in the dark for the sake of purity, young people would be encouraged to learn the skills and information they need in order to, say, prevent HIV or enjoy healthy, pleasurable sex lives.

Conclusion

As Katherine Angel writes in her lovely work *A Book on Desire, Most Difficult to Tell,* "Good loving can be fortuitous, partly a question of timing." Almost despite ourselves, she writes, we may find that "the lubricious body has run ahead, has jumped through the hoops, and gotten what it wanted." The opposite is also true: sometimes good sex evades us, despite our own valiant efforts (or those of our lovers).

Though good sex is never guaranteed, in a feminist utopia we would all be liberated and empowered to pursue our own erotic transcendence—and that's all we can really ask for. That, and maybe also, of course, "harder, harder," "yes," "more," and "right there."

Lori Adelman *is a writer and executive director of* Feministing, *where she creates and curates content on race, class, sex, gender, the media, and more. Lori is also a global advocacy and communications specialist, focusing on sexual and reproductive rights and health.*

Sliding Doors

JASMINE GIULIANI

This dossier prose poem was recently excavated from the Asymmetric Age of history and serves the wonderful purpose of allowing ethnographers to develop a study on an era that has been a subject of great disagreement amongst my colleagues in history departments across the country. Contextually speaking, the social echelon that I have focused on throughout this study was the middle-class, suburbanite, generation Y (circa those born between 1981 and 1994) female, during the first two decades of the 21st century. This small critique was the starting point of my wider analysis of an era of sexual oppression and gender inequality, which has now been largely dismantled in dominant culture. This artifact provides a very personal ancient perspective, rather than the statistical trends that have been available to us to date.

I clicked through a virtual gallery
of expectation
mutation
the women that beamed and squirmed
and grimaced in pain
they, a source from which I appraised myself
measuring my eagerness to
become a receptacle
measuring the markings of
a second pubescence
measuring the inherent width,
girth and elasticity

laying with my first boyfriend
my mantra like a shaman
upon the highest hill,
"swallow
shave
spread."

Author

Comment [1]: Whilst reading this historical prose poem, I have noted that the poet in question is referring to pornography, an archaic practice which has largely been shunned by the microcosms of society. Pornography was the visual portrayal of sexual matter for the purpose of arousal. At this time in history, prior to the passing of the Sexual Liberation Act of 2022 (SLA), pornography was a practice which objectified women and desensitized the public to images of male dominance and female coercion. Reflectively, this practice is unrecognizable compared to the visual imagery of sexuality now, which is produced by nonprofit institutions for educational purposes.

Author

Comment [2]: At this point in history, sexual objectification had become rather pedophilic and the practice of body mutation via shaving or waxing had proliferated a multibillion dollar industry. (As you may have noted, this was before the abolition of a singular monetary system in favor of the sustainable multieconomic system in place now.) This particular form of body modification has since become a respected but niche expression in society. The limited imagery which abounded in society at that time is now widely recognized by historians as a form of mass oppression and has been actively encouraged into a much more sexually diverse subgenrefied culture. Studies have shown a distinct link to the dismantling of mass media and the passing of Western epidemics like depression and anxiety.

My friend once referred to a vagina
as a chewed up
piece of hubba-bubba
I hope that mine is cute and
small and perfect
like a pet which I can name
models have cute pussies called
"Punani" and "Coochie"
I don't care if I am a model
I just hope I can do enough kegals
to not be a "Gash"
I suspect my vagina is a wound
I just don't want him to be afraid that
it will eat
the best parts of him
His body exhales and mine inhales
The first leg over the finish line
before each limb on the body
collapses after it

Author

Comment [3]: In the Assymetric Age the personification of the genitalia was used in many ways, to various effect. Now, of course, we call them ERO (external reproductive organs) and IRO (internal reproductive organs), both of which are fluid and are at the discretion of the identifier.

On top of a mini fridge after school
Two guys under a trampoline,
skewered, the party white noise
in her ears
which word is worse,
to hear in the common rooms
where doors slide
frigid

definition is a privilege unfairly bestowed
when can one define herself
when will the bell sound?

is he finished?
the only question that rings in the halls.

Author

Comment [4]: Since the passing of
the SLA, "shaming" and "demoral-
ization" based on sexual activity, or
lack thereof, has all but disappeared
from society. This dossier poem
demonstrates the potency of such
devices in forming nonconsensual
intercourse.

Author

Comment [5]: Many empirical
studies have shown that earlier
experiences of sexual intimacy
were heavily focused on the male
orgasm, which is in stark contrast to
the now common social practice of
simultaneous orgasm or device-aided
mutual gratification.

Jasmine Giuliani *had been a closet poet for around four years before getting the courage to share, submit, and workshop her poetry. Completing a degree in journalism has only taught her that she prefers to sieve this big place through poetry before she tastes it. She also likes dancing and eating, which are equal necessities.*

Interview with Judy Rebick

SHEILA HETI

The following is excerpted from an interview by Sheila Heti with Judy Rebick in October 2014. Heti is the author of six books, including the critically acclaimed novel How Should a Person Be? and the New York Times best seller Women in Clothes, a collaboration with Heidi Julavits and Leanne Shapton, featuring the voices of 639 women. She lives in Toronto. Judy Rebick is one of the most prominent feminists and voices of the left in Canada. Born in 1945, she was president of the National Action Committee on the Status of Woman, is the author of two books, and is the creator and former publisher of the popular news site rabble.ca.

I was thinking: in a utopia, you wouldn't have need for activism and you wouldn't have need for art.

Why?

Because a utopia is a perfect society, and activism exists to correct problems—but there wouldn't be any problems in a utopia. And art exists also because there are problems, even if they are only psychological or internal.

See, I don't think utopia is a perfect world. For me, utopia is a world where there is no oppression and there is no suffering and everyone is supported to do what they want to do, and what makes them happy. That, to me, is what a utopia is. But it doesn't mean there's no need for change, because a world without change would be dull. And a world without conflict of any kind would be dull. To me, utopia is a world that welcomes conflict. And you would still need activists. You'd still need the people who say, "Oh no, let's change this." It's human nature to want to change things. Young people are always challenging older people about the way they do things—like the way you see feminism and the way I see feminism is quite different. It's not 'cause there's something wrong with the way I see feminism, it's the nature of things that you grew up in a different environment than I did. And a world without art would be horrible.

But when you're defining utopia as a place without suffering—I think of people who want to change things because they witness suffering.

In our world that's true, but they could want to change things because things could be better, or different—or there could be a nicer way. Or they could come from a different part of the world and want to bring some of their culture. I don't think a utopia is a monoculture. There has to be different cultures, because you're not going to arrive at utopia by the domination of one culture over another. So there has to be diversity. And if there's diversity, then you're constantly learning and changing.

Where does your activism come from? I mean, specifically when you started becoming an activist and feminist.

Well, I'm a child of the sixties, so it was just cool to be an activist. And I didn't want to be what was expected of me as a woman. And at first I just thought that meant that I was more like men. Then, when I left university, I started to run into barriers—at work, you know. So I started to think more like a feminist. But it still took me a long time to become a feminist, because I thought feminists were anti-male, and I wasn't anti-male. But in the sixties, everybody was an activist. That's what was happening. All over the world—not just in Canada.

What can you compare it to now? Like the way it's cool to be active on the Internet now? Or being interested in having a conversation on Facebook or Twitter or online? It seemed that easy?

Yeah, in a way it was. But I think most people who were conscious in the sixties were activists. The thing about the music of the sixties—even the Beatles and the Stones, who were quite mainstream really—they had radical songs. Bob Dylan and Joan Baez and all the folk music was political. Music was our everything. Music was maybe what videos are now.

Right. Most of the feminists I know today who are effective in the world are artists. They don't make political statements as much. Their art is feminist and they are feminist, but they aren't joining with other women to go up against certain laws in the same way. They're not as politically active.

That's a reflection of neoliberal culture.

How's that?

Through the thirties and the Second World War, the excess of capitalism was tempered by the struggles of people. There began to be social programs—Medicare, welfare, unemployment insurance, a progressive tax system to redistribute wealth toward the poor. But all of that is either gone or severely weakened now, and the ideology that goes along with that weakening is a greater ideology of individualism, the idea that there are no collective solutions. Art is an individual solution. People think you can make a difference as an individual, not as a collective. Whereas I grew up in a time where everybody believed in collective solutions; that *we* could change the world. Power to the people.

Did you witness that change?

Yes, but I don't think we saw how deeply it would affect us. I think we foresaw the economic impacts, but we didn't foresee it changing ideologically. The cultural impact of neo-liberalism is the way it has isolated people. Of course, capitalism does that in general; it isolates people from each other, so there's less and less of a sense of community. The other day I was at the house of an old friend I've reconnected with—we were best friends when we were fourteen and I haven't seen her in fifty years. She asked me to come and speak to her women's group. I sit down with about ten women, and I have two sentences out of my mouth before they start asking me questions or engaging with me. It brought me back to a culture that I'm not part of anymore. You know, groups of women sitting around talking . . . my mother did that. She did it over mah-jongg, but it's the same thing! It didn't matter if we were talking politics or talking about a novel, we could be talking about somebody who's sick and wondering how to deal with it. It could be anything.

For no expressed purpose, you'd just get a bunch of women together to talk?

That's right. And that's really gone in this culture. I mean, people do it online, but it's not the same, right? You can build online relationships, but it's not the same as being in the same physical space.

Do you think it would change things a lot if more people again started having women's groups? Like, why don't I get you and Margaux and this artist and this person and this person together once every couple weeks, just to hang around and gab. Do you think that's important?

That is how the women's movement started. That's how the second wave started, with what we called consciousness-raising groups. We just sat around and gabbed and talked about our problems. My joke that I tell—when I speak—I say, "You know, we had a consciousness-raising group and then we found out it wasn't just *my* boyfriend who was an asshole, *everybody's* boyfriend was an asshole!" We learned that our individual problems were social problems.

Right.

That's a joke but that's really what happened. It's *really* what happened. I don't know if it could work now or not.

Why couldn't it? The first women's conscious-ness-raising group you were part of—how did it come together?

You just had friends in somebody's living room.

And how often would you meet with each other?

Once a week. I didn't do it a lot, but other women did. Then they said, "Well, we should do something about this." Let's say it was birth control. So then action came out of it. These were mostly students, so they did actions on campus with birth control information—

These were just people talking about their lives, and they realized, "Oh, the personal is political."

That's how we came to "the personal is political."

Because it's not just your life, others are having the same sort of experience.

That's right. One weakness in society now is that people don't reflect enough. Maybe that's not true for artists, but one of the problems with online communication is that it doesn't lead to reflection very much. It's too fast.

I imagine with these consciousness-raising groups that conversation could go anywhere and lead you to

the most interesting places. So, as unfuturistic as it seems, maybe we'd have more of these kinds of discussion groups in a utopia. How many people would there usually be?

It depends—there could be anywhere from five to twenty.

If consciousness-raising groups created second wave feminism, in part, and third wave feminism in part arose through the distribution of zines and conversations among women in bands going to see other women in bands . . .

Then activism *would* have a place in a feminist utopia because there would be conversations—more conversations and in more meaningful ways. Movements come from fighting injustice, but they can also come from people having conversations—not just at a head level, but at a heart level, too.

Welcome to Arcadia

JULIE ZEILINGER

We, the facilitators of Arcadia, are excited to welcome you to our new and improved contribution to the ever-expanding, vibrant feminist blogosphere.

Because the revolution happened so recently, this site may have changed since you were last here. Now, before you enter the site, please choose to log in as either a "writer" and offer your perspective on any given issue, or as a "listener and reader," and agree to actively engage and provide constructive feedback.

You are likely wondering why we have changed our log-in process. To learn more about the backstory behind these new changes (and to watch some of our favorite viral videos from the revolution, including the infamous feminist occupation of the Fox News Headquarters and the Men's Rights Activist Ostracization Ceremony) scroll down, or click next if you've been here before.

Scroll

Scroll

Many of us remember what it felt like to discover feminist blogging as it existed during the Age of Inequality. We believed it created an unprecedented, democratized space for a huge variety of feminists to claim their voices and be heard and influence the movement as well as the individuals within it.

However, now that we actually live in a feminist utopia, we know we weren't quite right. We now know that while exercising one's voice in the context of a society that seeks to silence it is undoubtedly vital, this uproar can't exist alone.

Yes, previously marginalized women had an unprecedented opportunity to speak and be visible in the feminist blogosphere, but their privileged counterparts still took up much of that space. As we saw for years, the most privileged actors in the feminist movement often spoke over and on behalf of those who needed to drive the conversation, whether intentionally or unintentionally, from a place of paternalistic superiority or from an unrecognized, unchecked sense of entitlement. No matter the intentions, the result was damaging: many of us were speaking, but we were not heard equally. Few of us were really, truly listening.

Though we now collectively understand the distinction between when it's appropriate to vocalize one's ideas, in our own community as well as in public, and when it's necessary to exercise silence in a radical way—and that the two must be clearly delineated—it is of course still easy to lose sight of these goals. We must not forget that the core of online feminism is voice: who is being heard, in what capacity, and at what volume.

We must remember that without tempering who speaks and when, the same dynamics that marginalized those individuals and their agendas are again reinscribed.

This is why we're writing this note: to remind you, readers and writers of Arcadia, that taking care of this community by attentively and actively listening is a necessary and vigilant form of activism and is essential to making sure the power differentials of our society's sexist past don't reemerge. Even though we've equalized society, we must consciously continue to theorize listening as an imperative act in our online spaces. Spaces of equality can't magically materialize out of enthusiasm or good intentions, but they can be actively constructed by striking a balance of voice. Our feminist revolution has never been purely additive. It has never *just* been about creating *more* space for previously marginalized voices (although, this has, of course, been vital). We must continue to match the creation of space for those who have been historically marginalized with purposeful restraint by others. Since the revolution, individuals have learned to understand when it is appropriate and necessary for them to be silent so that others can speak and really be *heard.* We have cut to the heart and soul of feminism's purpose and we honor the integrity of the overall movement. And we must continue to do so.

This balance has always been far easier demanded than enacted but the following guiding principles of this blog will allow us to shape these demands into our reality:

Users, as well as facilitators of this site, are paid fair wages for their work based on the government resources allocated to social justice efforts.

Our highly sophisticated monitoring mechanism limits the number of posts each user contributes every month and sends messages encouraging participation to hesitant community members.

Diversity of all users is not tokenistically manufactured here—this is an accessible space. Writers will not be paraded for the various ways in which you represent diverse factions. You will speak for yourselves and your own experiences, choosing only to reveal your personal background if it's relevant to your work.

Because we understand that it is also essential to honor individuals' pride in their difference, to acknowledge a very real history of discrimination based on that difference, and to make sure all users are comfortable, there are specific support groups based on various factors of commonality available to users, so that you are not defined by, but still feel supported in, your difference.

With these guiding principles in mind, we can't wait to hear your voices and read the opinions you will offer, and we hope you can't wait to actively listen and absorb the opinions and voices of others.

Happy blogging!

Your Editorial Collective

Julie Zeilinger *is the founder and editor of the* FBomb, *a feminist blog and community for young adults partnered with the Women's Media Center. Julie has been named one of* Newsweek's *"150 Women Who Shake the World," one of* Woman's Day's *"8 Influential Bloggers under 21," and one of the* London Time's *"40 Bloggers Who Really Count." She is the author of two books:* A Little F'd Up: Why Feminism Is Not a Dirty Word *and* College 101: A Girl's Guide to Freshman Year.

Interview with Mia McKenzie

The following is excerpted from an interview an edi-tor conducted over the phone with writer and cultural critic Mia McKenzie on August 12, 2014. McKenzie is a writer, a speaker, and a smart, scrappy Philadelphian with a deep love of black feminism and fake fur collars. Her first novel, *The Summer We Got Free*, won the 2013 Lambda Literary Award. She is the creator of *Black Girl Dangerous*, a website that amplifies the voices of queer and trans people of color.

So much of your writing is about questions of who gets to speak for whom on what issues. I'm wondering how you think the role of the public intellectual would be different in a feminist utopia? Would that role exist at all? How would it be different? How would your career be different in that world?

I probably wouldn't have to write [my blog *Black Girl Dangerous (BGD)*] in my feminist utopia. In the utopia, everyone would just have what they need and marginalized voices would already be heard. In a utopia I could just write novels. When people ask what I do, I always say I write fiction, because that's what I love. But the other writing I do, like [political and cultural criticism] for *BGD*, is from a sense that it's needed and urgent. In a utopia I could focus on the writing that is more important to me on a personal level.

Do you think fiction would change as well?

It would probably change in some ways, but I would still definitely tell stories about communities that I am a part of and the people I know and love. Their experiences are very personal and important to me.

But maybe the ways in which it was needed would change. We could focus more on the beauty of our stories, just the telling of them, just the sharing of them, just the healing and the joy and all the things that come with sharing stories. We could think of our writing less as a tool and more just as sharing.

To shift focus a little bit: You've criticized the butch/ femme dichotomy in queer dating scenes but also have celebrated the bold performativity of certain queer expression or exaggerations of gender—I don't

get the impression that in your utopia there's a uniform androgyny. I know this is a big question, maybe an unfair question, but I'm wondering what you think gender would be in a feminist utopia.

I think that people would have more access to performing gender or claiming gender than they do now. I definitely don't see androgyny as the standard in a feminist utopia. I see femininity not being policed, femininity not being thought of as less than, and also people having access to express themselves in whatever ways they wanted to. I don't see eliminating labels around gender because a lot of people identify strongly with certain genders. I see more access to more choices, more possibilities, more fluidity, and fewer boxes.

Along those lines—the fewer boxes—in a lot of your writing you refer to this refrain of "getting free." At its core, what does getting free mean?

That's a huge question for me. Marginalized people get stuck in the stories that other people tell about us in a way that holds us back. Getting free means accessing our full humanity. It's not that these things, the experiences of being oppressed, aren't real or aren't happening: they're completely real and true. But I'm talking about what we make those things mean about ourselves and our communities, and how we relate to each other. For example, we often get stuck in stories about bad things that happened to us as children. And it's not that those things didn't happen, and that the traumas we experienced aren't real. They're real. But what we do is make what happened mean something about who we are.

A youth I worked with, a queer youth of color, was told as a child that she was "so dark." She was just a little girl, and what she made this mean about herself was that she was ugly and unwanted. She carried around that story— that she was ugly and unwanted—for the next decade. Every time she turned on the TV or opened a magazine, it was reinforced by society. It affected not only how she felt about herself, but also the ways that she related to people. Even when she was wanted, she couldn't see it. She was always waiting for proof that she wasn't. She didn't think she could be loved or desired or respected. It wasn't until she was able to understand that this was a story that she had made up—not that this hadn't been said about her, not that colorism wasn't real, but that what she'd accepted that it meant about herself wasn't real—that she was able to get free of that story and live a life where she wasn't held back by the idea that she was unwanted. And she was able to recognize all of the people who had loved and wanted and respected her throughout her young life. I had her make a list and it was long. The story had kept her from accessing her full humanity as a person who could have relationships where she felt loved, and could return love.

When we get to utopia, we'll still carry our communities' histories with us, right? How would you like to see us handle these experiences and stories?

I'd hope to see us retelling and processing those histories in ways that heal those past traumas for those who experienced them. That means decentralizing the "education" of others and focusing on the emotional, psychological, physical, and mental benefits to be gained from processing those histories by those who had to endure them.

Beyond Badass
Toward a Feminist, Antiracist Literature

DANIEL JOSÉ OLDER

I was on a panel of science fiction editors the other day and we were discussing what tropes we're tired of seeing. "It's not enough," editor Rose Fox said, "that a woman be badass." Rose and I edited the anthology *Long Hidden: Speculative Fiction from the Margins of History* together and I knew exactly what they were talking about. Even in a collection of stories explicitly dedicated to unraveling oppression and stereotypes, our slush pile was full of women characters that were either passive and in need of saving or simply badass and nothing else.

Yes, we want badass women in literature! Absolutely. But *badass* so often comes at the cost of their greater humanity; it turns into their singular trait. We don't allow women space outside strict dichotomies; we don't allow them in between. This is particularly true when it comes to black women, whom writers tend to portray as either asexual or hypersexual, on top of the already simplified passive and badass extremes. None of these tropes describe a fully formed, complex person. Here, at the intersection of race and gender clichés, we must challenge ourselves to do better. As womanist, writer, and social critic Trudy writes on her blog *Gradient Lair*:

> I feel the most powerful when I feel the most self-acceptably complex and this means the space to thrive and be without misogynoiristic demands for performance of or desire for some rigid myth of Black women's "empowerment" look like . . . My empowerment looks like my humanity, and my humanity is my focus, with all of its history, nuance, complexity.

It's not enough to simply invert a stereotype: flipping the script on the passive damsel in distress still plays into the same simplistic dichotomy. A true counter-narrative breaks out of the structures that had confined it by committing to the fullness of its own messy truths. Our struggles to resist oppression, our very identities in this war-torn world, are far too multilayered and nuanced to fit in the narrow boxes that clichés try to squeeze us into. We need protagonists who are more than just badasses or damsels: we need women characters that are humans.

A truly feminist, antiracist literary world will go beyond being badass. I imagine walking down aisles and aisles of books one day: a plethora of science fiction and fantasy covers with women heroes of all different races, shapes, sizes; romance covers with LGBTQ relationships; children's books will show many models of gender beyond the binary. I imagine a literary world that will explore dimensions of womanhood that are multiracial and trans-inclusive. It will challenge notions of patriarchal masculinity and heteronormativity. And most of all, it will be rich with fully formed, vivid characters, pulsing with vitality and their messy, beautiful truths.

When literature moves into a dynamically feminist stance, the world will transform with it. We will see children growing up in a world that is much more unburdened by sexism, and in turn their imaginations will churn out a new generation of literary arts. A new story will begin.

Daniel José Older *is the author of* Half-Resurrection Blues *(book one of the Bone Street Rumba urban fantasy series from Penguin's Roc Books) and the upcoming Young Adult novel* Shadowshaper *(Scholastic's Arthur A. Levine Books, 2015). You can find his thoughts on writing, read dispatches from his decade-long career as an NYC paramedic, and hear his music at ghoststar.net, on YouTube, and @djolder on Twitter.*

Interview with Chloe Angyal

The following is excerpted from an interview an editor conducted with writer and media expert Dr. Chloe Angyal over the phone on October 1, 2014. Angyal is an opinion writer for Reuters, *senior editor at* Feministing, *and a senior facilitator at the OpEd Project. She had just completed her media studies doctoral dissertation on romantic comedies when we spoke. Part of her work for her PhD was watching (pretty much) every English-language rom-com ever made from a feminist angle. Angyal has some ideas about the importance of these films and how they could be improved.*

Would there be rom-coms in utopia?

Absolutely. Romantic comedies are about important human questions: love, family, friendship, work, belonging, sacrifice. The reason rom-coms persist in this nonfeminist nonutopia is that we are all deeply concerned with those ideas. In a feminist utopia, we would still need to explore all those things. But rom-coms would look very different than they do now.

Honestly, I think there would be fewer "happy" endings. In rom-coms now, it's only a happy ending if the couple ends up together. And we know that in real life, sometimes you don't end up with the person you had a love story with, and yet you're both happy. In a feminist utopia, you'd have realistic romantic comedies, which means a lot of couples not ending up together. That doesn't mean the love is any less valuable, any less meaningful, any less life changing, any less heart shaping—but you break up because that's how a lot of happy relationships work.

Rom-coms where people end up together would also look very, very different. For one thing, there would be less of people shutting each other up by kissing. Shakespeare did it in *Much Ado About Nothing*. You should never silence someone by putting your mouth on their mouth. It's not a great way to get consent; it's not a great way to honor what someone's trying to say.

I also think you'd have people coming together—if they do come together—in a way that feels egalitarian and authentic. I think we've all had the experience of watching a rom-com and thinking "these people are totally wrong for each other." The story tries to convince us, though, that the fact that they're totally mismatched, in really fundamental ways that threaten the core of who they are, means they're perfect for each other. The career woman and the misogynist is a classic. In a feminist utopia, you'd see couples that really work well together, who respect each other, and don't just shut each other up with a kiss. Then, you as a viewer could be genuinely happy for them.

What replaces the kiss?

There's no such thing as perfectly feminist pop culture, or at least not yet, but at the end of *Friends with Benefits*, a 2011 movie starring Justin Timberlake and Mila Kunis, there is a feminist grand gesture. He puts on a flash mob for her in Grand Central, they pour their hearts out to each other, and there is what scholars call the "key kiss"—the kiss that consummates the relationship. Every rom-com has that. In this movie they do that, and then they walk out and go sit at a restaurant and talk. You get a sense of what their relationship might actually look like after the key kiss.

And it looks a lot like their relationship before the key kiss. Rom-coms say that your relationship is going to be magically transformed by your decision to be together forever, which is what the key kiss symbolizes. So if he's been awful up until now, suddenly everything will be better—but we know from the very real statistics about intimate partner abuse and domestic violence that that's not how it works. *Friends with Benefits* gets that: it depicts a relationship that is basically the same before and after the kiss.

We have certain myths and fantasies about romance that we find attractive and so they end up in movies, and then we find them attractive because we see them in movies. What would be good feminist myths for the utopia? What stories would we tell that would send positive messages?

The screenwriter Aline Brosh McKenna is really good at telling stories about relationships between women, which is pretty transgressive. I particularly like *Morning Glory*, where the lead character continually says, "I love my job. I'm good at my job. I refuse to be shamed for that." Most of the contemporary rom-coms tell you that because she's good at her job she's bad at her love life. I think in a feminist utopia, we would keep telling stories about women in the real world who are good at lots of things, and defined by lots of characteristics, and who refuse to apologize for their complexity.

What would real-life dating look like in a feminist utopia?

There'd be a lot less rape. In fact, there'd be no rape. Who pays for the first date would no longer be an issue because we'd all agree we should split the check fifty-fifty, and it would actually be fifty-fifty because women would get equal pay for equal work. Right now, I'm happy to split the bill and have the guy pay for the tip, a sexism surcharge. I'm not kidding. I actually went on a date with a guy once who made that joke and I thought, "You get a second date just for that."

You would not be defined by the gender identity of the people that you dated and you would not define yourself by the physical attractiveness and income of the people you dated. Your value in the dating market would not be defined by what kind of job you have, how much money you make, or what you look like. This sounds so incredibly far-fetched and yet I want it so badly.

What would a perfect Friday night date look like in a rom-com made in a feminist utopia?

Dates look so performative in rom-coms right now. I feel like this answer is going to morph into "What is Chloe's ideal Friday night date?"

Okay, so: Chloe Angyal, what are we going to do if I take you out in a feminist utopia?

Gosh. It should involve very good conversation and some sexual chemistry—whether acted on or not—and that's obviously tied in pretty strongly to the intellectual chemistry. In a feminist utopia, everyone knows that intelligence is sexy, and that it's *complementary* intelligence that's the sexiest thing of all. It's not just that someone's smart, but that they're the kind of smart that works with your kind of smart.

And we'd have some whiskey.

Poems for Past Lovers 1-3

CHARLOTTE LIEBERMAN

I wrote these poems using the language, ideas, feelings, and structures from emails written to me by three past lovers. The emails I chose as the subjects for this piece struck me as particularly frustrating at the time I received them, and still do today. Their obscure language felt coded, hegemonically masculine, emotionally abstruse—uncannily strong and stoic in a way that seemed to reinforce "the legitimacy of patriarchy," securing "the dominant position of men and the subordination of women," to quote R.W. Connell's pivotal work *Masculinities*.

When thinking about why these relationships failed, there is an unsurprising answer: poor communication. Sure, my communication with each of these men was also poor in the context of text messages, sporadic phone calls, and in person. But the medium of email seemed to be a particularly fertile starting place for this project, as it is so often the site of oblique and unproductive flirtation, manipulation, and evasion. More than any other mode of communication, email is an intricate craft. Or, as Miranda July explained to the *Rumpus* in an interview about her recent project "We Think Alone," which finds a different way to use email as its primary medium, "[Email]'s something where you do your end of it totally alone, and you can make it perfect." In short, I wanted to open up these wrought, heavily crafted messages at their seams. I wanted to feel, as I would in my feminist utopia, a sense of actual exchange, emotional "intercourse," in the language.

I've reauthored these emails, inhabiting the voices of past lovers in an attempt to turn what I saw (and still see) as a dysfunctional, detached, yet hyperguarded mode of communicating into one that is unabashed in its expression of care, desire, pain, and more. This gesture unto itself feels definitionally utopic: in a process of emotional alchemy, I turned impersonal and aloof prose into a poetic outlet for a creative expression of something personal and cathartic.

My intention: to rewrite, retell, and recover. For me and for the feminist utopia.

FOR LOVER #1

The Toilet Incident

I forgot to give it
to you again but there
is no need for
me to offer you

an apology. Here

it is! Definitely
let me know what
you hear. Tues-
day? Good

luck. I
am not in Utah
right now, but
if I were, I would

not tell you that
coffee some time
soon would be
great. I would

tell you *Tuesday.*
I am telling you
Tuesday. There is
no need

to wish you
good luck.

FOR LOVER #2

Trust Me

I am coming back at the end

of May.
I am

good. I
am sure.

We can break
bread.

FOR LOVER #3

On responding to your emails
promptly and thoughtfully

My dad and I were out and
about traveling and I did

take my phone and I did not
say *sorry about that* because

I did not need to. I got your
texts before this morning

and I read them and I asked
questions like *how did you like*

your dinner, was it hot enough
for you

and I cared. I care about what
you have been doing, not about

how your final went. I did not ask
did your final go well

because frankly you are
probably not thinking about it

anymore now that it's over, nor
are you thinking about me.

I have been doing more than
very little, more than reading,

watching movies, sleeping,
mostly sleeping

actually.

Charlotte Lieberman *is a New York-based poet and essayist who likes to write about feminism, the digital economy, millennials, literature, food, and wellness.*

Interview with Suey Park

The following is excerpted from an interview the editors conducted with activist Suey Park via phone and email over the course of the fall of 2014. Park is passionate about women of color, feminism, and digital media and is the cofounder of Killjoy Prophets, a collective committed to ending Dudebro Christianity. The nation followed her 2014 campaign to #CancelColbert, which garnered hundreds of thousands of tweets and retweets and raised important questions about media power and who gets to decide what's funny. Park agreed to chat with us about a big question: Who gets to feel?

What would our emotional lives look like in a feminist utopia?

In a feminist utopia, a wider range of emotional expression would be tangible. Right now, we police our own behaviors, feelings, and image in a world where being a woman comes with having the undue responsibility to earn respect before having concerns heard—let alone considered.

Although we may espouse a disloyalty to the very structures that subjugate us through the rejection of patriarchal ideals and the decentering of whiteness, I believe our obedience to the system is still in operation with regards to our emotional lives even when fighting these systems. We withhold and internalize our pain—turning it inward. Since when did being a strong leader mean choking back tears? In the contemporary world, we see pressure to overcome and to always suffer silently.

And we justify the logics of abuse when we instrumentalize the harms we've suffered to promote a larger cause. Rape, trauma, heartbreak, and betrayal become narratives sold to win campaigns. A victim calls herself a survivor to dignify violence that cannot be dignified. A "well-packaged" story illustrating rape culture on a personal level gets told and retold. Since when did becoming an activist have a prerequisite of trauma? I want to live in a world where suffering isn't glorified.

In a feminist utopia, pain will continue to exist. However, we will rely less on western rationalism and western medicine to dictate appropriate timelines for healing or appropriate ways to heal. Perhaps in a feminist utopia, my "hysteria" might be affirmed. It may be diagnosed as "the world hurt you with its sickness" rather than "you are sick."

In a utopia, healing wouldn't be simply about individualized narratives of "getting over it," but rather a collective response to remove the very source of pain from ever injuring one of our own again.

Even among feminist circles, I hear so many women "tone police" one another—silencing people by attacking their [vehemence or volume] and ignoring the substance of what they are saying, always insisting that we should respond more calmly, more rationally, to keep people comfortable rather than truly expressing ourselves. This policing of behavior is a form of surveillance—a form of patriarchal gatekeeping. It's concerning that when we do show emotions people are so quick to label that as "crazy," which is of course stigmatizing, which is of course limiting. Emotions are part of being alive and human.

The last time we talked you mentioned that in a feminist utopia, we wouldn't have to worry that the love or the loss we feel over a breakup is the result of false consciousness—that we could honor our feelings as real, even as we understand socialization.

My friends at the poetry group Dark Matter always call this "America's Next Top Radical," when people think their emotions are only valid if they can back it up with a political argument. It's a shame people get so caught up in performing our radical politics and intellect. In a feminist utopia, you'd be able to say, "hey, I'm jealous because I am human" or "you hurt me" without having to develop a critique. Being held accountable for hurting someone or getting away with causing hurt should not be dependent on one person's ability to out-critique the other.

How would this look different in a feminist utopia?

I would hope that when people go through breakups there would be more support. We would no longer worry about seeming antifeminist in mourning the loss of a partner, especially a male partner. A lot of what I do is motivated by not wanting to conform to a stereotype. However, the pressure to not conform to a stereotype is just as damaging as the pressure to conform to one. "How can I be in a relationship as a feminist and not be too dependent? Am I in love or am I seduced by patriarchy into feeling comfortable and happy? And am I heartbroken because it was real or because I feel pressure to have a male partner?"

A relationship ending is real loss. Someone might go from being your "everything" to being your nothing in the blink of an eye. It doesn't matter if you know the romance myth—the idea that there is one all-consuming true love who will complete our lives—is unhealthy. The loss is still real. I went through a couple terrible breakups and I wondered if those people had ever been with me truly. I don't know if it's true for you, too, but given the price of being a "tough" feminist and activist, it becomes all the more important to have people in my intimate bubble—my self-made utopia—who see me for who I am and know they will stay by my side.

In a feminist utopia, people wouldn't say, "You'll get over it" or, "You were too good for him." Instead, there would be a lot of acknowledging and mourning loss. Rather than wanting a quick fix, I would hope in a feminist utopia folks would ask, "What do you think you are missing now without your partner?" or "What does your breakup trigger for you?" in order to begin to fill in the missing pieces collectively and begin to make sense of a more stable way to do relationships. Yes, the romance myth is dangerous. Yes, there might not be "one" person out there for us. Act in ways that offer alternatives to the romwance myth, while still offering healing for those experiencing heartbreak.

The fact that we can psychoanalyze *why* people react to gender violence and the romance myth doesn't make those responses any less real. We still hurt.

I'm struck that in your conception, even in the perfect society we would still experience grief and loss as part of being human—but we're allowed it in a more intimate way, and more on our terms.

It is unrealistic to think pain would cease to exist in a feminist utopia. I know for me, the goal is not to be happy all the time. The goal is to be able to better cope with the pain that comes with life. A lot of times our pain merely increases when it is not affirmed and allowed to run its course. The goal is not to become emotionally repressive. Our pain, our tears, our sweat, our laughter tell us something. It may tell us something unjust has happened that cannot be ignored nor forgotten.

Crazy Bitches
Redefining Mental Health (Care) in the Feminist Utopia

TESSA SMITH

Perhaps the only difference between me and other people was that I've always demanded more from the sunset, more spectacular colors when the sun hit the horizon . . . that's perhaps my only sin.
— Joe (Charlotte Gainsbourg), *Nymphomaniac*, 2013

You might call me a movie masochist. Devastating, depressing, and potentially scarring, my after-dinner Netflix selections have been known to bring the party down. On my way home from one such round of filmic self-flagellation (a screening of Lars von Trier's *Dogville*[1]), failing to process the barrage of blurred thoughts and emotions that had unleashed itself as soon as the credits started to roll, I stepped off the curb into the street. My manic preoccupation had rendered me pretty indifferent to the amount of traffic, its

[1]. If you plan on watching it (and you should), please do so in your living room with loving, supportive friends.

speed, or its trajectory. Luckily for me, this earned me an eleven-day trip to the closest psychiatric hospital as opposed to the OR, or for that matter, the morgue.

Despite assurances from friends that those nights shivering under thin hospital blankets listening to the midnight chorus of grunts and wails or the daily lunchtime farce of having to eat dry chicken breasts with a plastic spoon would one day yield a best-selling memoir, my takeaways from that ordeal have, thus far, been more political and academic than literary. My experiences with the world of mental health care in America then and since have exposed a system that is predominantly paternalistic, at times sadistic, and, occasionally anachronistic. The word "hysteria," or at least "hysterical" (as in, "we can't discuss the possibility of your discharge while you're this hysterical"), came up several times in both inpatient and outpatient interactions with MDs, social workers, and therapists. Whether it's the Hippocratic theory of a dehydrated, drifting womb wreaking havoc around the body—the Victorian ladies' malady thought to be curable with a well-placed water cannon—or Freud's analysis of medically inexplicable psychosomatic symptoms, *hysteria* is a concept loaded with centuries of gender-specific ideas of mental health. Even when the word itself was absent, hysteria was there, lurking between the lines of evaluation reports: a silent diagnosis. *Nurse! Orderly! Somebody catch that wandering uterus!*

Much of the bitter anger I felt (and feel) for the doctors responsible for those early days of my treatment stemmed from being denied a voice in the discussion of my own health, in a way that felt inseparable from the gendered lens through which they (falsely) perceived my condition. The experts eventually settled on a bipolar II diagnosis, but it was clear that I had been triaged before my arrival into the category of the worn-out, frail-nerved college coed whose inability to handle the intellectual rigors of an elite education had resulted in a breakdown and suicide attempt. The only other college student in the ward while I was there (like the friend of a friend whom I later found out had been through the system earlier) was female; and virtually all of my fellow inpatients fell into one or more of the key categories (female, nonwhite, immigrant, queer, trans, gender-fluid or ambiguous, poor, poorly educated, living with mental or physical disabilities, homeless, veteran) that make up the vast, silenced segment of the population that is oppressed by the capitalist patriarchy.

Access to quality psychiatric care and psychotherapy, a less misogynist medical vocabulary, and a more patient-centered type of care are absolutely imperative; however, this kind of change would do little to disrupt the mission of today's psychiatry to the radical degree that a feminist utopia demands. Mental health care as we know it is mostly centered on the principle of maintaining mental and emotional stability. For the people who experience emotional and mental states that extend beyond the normative range, "treatment" largely means changing the ways they experience the world to come into line with the socially accepted norm. The exception to this is the extremely gendered, race- and class-biased cliché of the "brilliant, sensitive eccentric" that society is all too willing to accept within the category of the white, middle or upper-class male.

What if every "crazy bitch" or "psycho" was valued as much as the "eccentric"? How would the world change if we cast our horizons further than the moderate changes described above? What if states of mind that extend beyond the norm were nurtured instead of inhibited? Acknowledging people with extraordinary mental and emotional perspectives as not only valid but also *valuable* members of society, not despite but because of their exceptional mental and emotional conditions, is a key element of an ideal feminist society. Support, not suppression, should be the principle on which we base our mental health care. The culture of the feminist utopia must be one in which people experiencing extraordinary mental states can both survive *and* thrive.

I want to be clear: This is not to deny the fact that mental illness—as illness qua sickness—is absolutely real, to the extent that it can prevent people from living the lives that they want for themselves in safety, if not cause them to lose touch with reality altogether (all of which I've seen and will not forget in a hurry). Mental illnesses are very often deadly, but a balance must always be struck between keeping patients suffering extreme mental pain or dangerous delusions safe and giving them autonomy over their own lives. With this in mind, pharmaceutical care, as a part of a cooperative treatment plan between patient and psychiatrist, must still be considered a viable part of the emotionally inclusive culture of the feminist utopia. The difference between the current state of mental health care and the kind we hope to create is that states of mind that extend beyond the average spectrum will not be suppressed or "cured" but, rather, provided with the best possible environments in which they can be experienced.

As it stands, we live in a system in which psychological conditions are pathologized while being treated, perversely, in the least healthy environments imaginable. Sending a manic or depressed (or schizophrenic, or aggressive, or anxious) person to a typical psych ward is like sending someone who has just suffered a heart attack to recuperate in an improvised military hospital in the middle of an air raid. Ever the German literature major, I had half-seriously imagined the "hospital" as some urban equivalent of an alpine sanatorium à la Thomas Mann, with muesli-munching patients taking in the salubrious air while sunning themselves in deck chairs and playing chess. What I had in fact signed up for was eleven days without exercise or fresh air; nutritionally devoid, fatty, sugary food; and a prevailing state of general tension.[2]

In a feminist utopia, instances when inpatient care

2. The only exception: my expectations felt momentarily justified when I became the unofficial Jenga champion of a ward filled with addicts with shaky withdrawal-hands.

is necessary would be structured to be as beneficial to the patients' states of mind as possible. Access to exercise is imperative; nutrition, of course, equally so. Most importantly, emphasis would be shifted from teaching patients techniques for suppressing their extraordinary mental states to helping each individual find the best ways for her to thrive. "Prescriptions" as a part of mental health care in the feminist utopia, both pharmaceutical and nonpharmaceutical, must not be *pro*scriptive; the authority and agency of each patient in her own care would be acknowledged and incorporated.

The withholding of autonomy from mental health patients—especially in the context of hospitalization—is a manifestation of the notion that a "mentally ill" individual is incapable of making decisions, not just as a patient but also as a citizen. Women, "hysterical" and otherwise, are particularly at risk of this kind of disempowerment. States of mind that don't conform to the normative standard of happiness are seen as undesirable and unacceptable because they are at odds with the great lie of capitalism: that life is nothing but the individual pursuit of happiness and that the measure of that happiness is money. Any state of mind that is out of line with the agreed-on principle that happiness is the human default is seen as a sickness that must be cured, just as any person who exists in a manner inconsistent with the bourgeois status quo is a blight on society at best and a terrorist at worst.

As late as 2002, twenty-six years after the death in

prison of Ulrike Meinhof—one of the most prominent members of the West German extreme-left terrorist group, the Rote Armee Fraktion (RAF)—an examination of Meinhof's brain was undertaken in an effort to prove that the former journalist could not be held criminally culpable for her part in the RAF's acts of terror: that the true culprit was an emotional imbalance caused by damage to the limbic system she had sustained during an operation in 1962.[3] Regardless of whether or not a brain injury can be responsible for one's ideologies, the case exemplifies our society's desire to neutralize the political woman. Women's expressions of dissatisfaction with the existing system—particularly when violent—are dismissed as manifestations of irrationality or emotional instability rather than political conviction. Whether a uterus on the loose or a bruised brain, a woman's body continues to be seen as the dictator of her actions. Acknowledging that the expression of sadness, dissatisfaction, and anger is valid would undermine the very idea that drives and justifies the capitalist social structure.

People who are more in touch with suffering and ecstasy than the majority are not a hindrance in imagining the feminist utopia—they are a resource. The critical states of mind that come with depression can facili-

3. A story about the research was published in popular German magazine, *Der Spiegel* under the somewhat "hysterical" title "RAF: The Brain of Terror" (Jürgen Dahlkamp. "RAF: Das Gehirn des Terrors." Spiegel Online. *Der Spiegel*, 8 Nov. 2002. Web. 30 Sep. 2014.)

tate an understanding of what is wrong with the world, which—along with the sensitivity, creativity, and energy associated with certain kinds of mania—is so vital to both artistic and political action. To avoid losing valuable utopian thinkers, we need to abandon the system—both the capitalist patriarchy itself and its medical right hand—that suppresses unhappiness and blunts the edge of passion. As the filmmaker Rainer Werner Fassbinder[4] was well aware, inability to feel despair can lead to dangerous complacency: "It's precisely those people who don't have any reasons, any motivation, any despair, any utopia, who can easily be used by others."[5] The most disruptive thing in our struggle toward utopia is not the cry of despair or the unbroken shout of excitement but the silence of a gagged mouth.

Reforming our attitudes toward extraordinary mental and emotional states not only affects the practice of psychiatry but also is a vital step on the way to freeing up every voice silenced by oppression. Once we have removed one of the key principles on which the capital-

4. R.W. Fassbinder (1945-1982) is one of my academic obsessions and a definite guest at my fantasy dead people dinner party. His extraordinary mind gave birth to (roughly) forty feature-length films, three shorts, two TV series', twenty-four stage plays, thirty-six acting roles, and various other projects – in less than fifteen years. That alone could kill you by the age of thirty-seven, even if your lifestyle doesn't include chain-smoking and copious doses of cocaine and barbiturates.

5. Rainer Werner Fassbinder. "'I've changed along with the characters in my films': A Discussion with Hella Schlumberger about Work and Love, the Exploitability of Feelings, and the Longing for Utopia." in *The Anarchy of the Imagination: Interviews, Essays, Notes*. Eds. Michael Töteberg and Leo A. Lensing, trans. Krishna Winston. Baltimore: Johns Hopkins University Press, 1992, 37.

ist patriarchy is built—that happiness, or rather, docility, is the only valuable state of mind—then it will start to topple and, eventually, come crashing down. To redefine our world, we must redefine what mental health should be. What the patriarchy condemns as sins, the feminist utopia celebrates as virtues: expressing our despair, voicing our dissatisfaction, unleashing the full force of our imaginations, demanding more from the sunset.

Tessa Smith *is based in Berlin, Germany. Her current work (funded by a 2014–2015 Fulbright scholarship) focuses on gender and spectatorship in German visual art and film.*

No Escape Hatch

RIA FAY-BERQUIST

One morbidly humid August evening in 2000, during the third week of a cross-country road trip, I stepped into a telephone booth in Rapid City, South Dakota to make a call. The recipient of the phone call is actually of little import: no one answered. Instead, I very quickly turned around to find that the accordion-door phone booth had been sealed shut by a husky boy my age leaning his body up against it, and by the looks on his friends' faces in the near distance, grinning. I tried pushing the glass door open, and then, operating as if I were in on the joke, and not disabled by confusion, regret, and the fear that this was a potential fork in the road that I might not travel back from, let out a small forced laugh, and something like, "very funny, let me out."

Cheryl Strayed, in *Wild*, her memoir about hiking the Pacific Crest Trail alone, expertly encapsulates my next several moments inside the booth:

I could hardly hear my own words for what felt like a great clanging in my head, which was the realization that my whole [trip] could come to this. That no matter how tough or strong or brave I'd been, how comfortable I'd come to be with being alone, I'd also been lucky, and that if my luck ran out now, it would be as if nothing before it had ever existed, that this one evening would annihilate all those brave days.

Moments later, as his friends approached, the boy leaned off the doors, and the group paraded past, banging on the telephone booth, laughing, and hollering. I didn't hear their words, the ringing in my ears drowning out every peak and valley from consonant to vowel. I stood woodenly alone, the door to the booth fluttering open, as if the boys had been a desaturated mirage, wondering if in fact this had really happened—at dusk, with plenty of streetlights, in the parking lot of a Denny's. The negotiation between the near indigestible fact of rogue aggression and its mundane backdrop is one of the many dissonant facets of being female, and female on the road.

The remainder of the trip became a subtle yet simmering power struggle between my female travel companion and I. I, having been born of a family that was defined by a legacy of violence—political, familial, and a fair share of random acts—could not talk myself into the fantasy that I was beyond its reach. In large part, an impending attack felt like my destiny, my fate. A hazing ritual that would leave me branded and identified as part of "our clan," with the primal knowledge that so far had eluded me in most respects. My friend, waiting in the car on the other side of the parking lot, refused to allow four young strangers to determine any part of our outcome as women traveling alone. She did not want to pair up with a group of Australian backpackers just for protection. She spoke theoretically about male power and our right to be here, and I shook my head, albeit internally, at what I perceived as naiveté and a battle not worth the win; her lush landscape in contrast to my desert, contaminated by history that was not my own. I wanted to be brave and so I decided, as I would decide many times to come in my future of travel, that I could stop and be afraid, and my fear would determine the scope of my life, or I could continue the course.

This is the transaction we make as women, a bargaining with fate to allow us an inch of restricted freedom, at the cost of an assumed risk. As women travelers, and women off of the grid, we are vigilant in our assessment of our environments, constantly identifying our escape hatch: if they try to ____, I will ____ with ____. The armor of observation and readiness carries us into the wild. When we go unscathed, the world around us is perceived as just. When we do not, we didn't listen and it is our fault and our fate.

Consciously or not, we have internalized these laws, and policed our own (and others') desires accordingly. A show of camaraderie for women traveling alone is rare. Instead, women are encouraged to be reliant on male protection, whether or not the men in question are pre-pared or able to offer it.

Men have certain latitudes and a definite mythol-ogy to draw on when it comes to lone discoveries—of far-reaching territories, of the origins of humankind, of oneself. We might pass a compass and a map to a young man as a rite of passage—but to a woman? And yet women also require latitude. We require solitude, retreat, wing-span, and uncharted movement, communion within the elements without the static of artifice and the guardrails of a program or agenda.

In imagining a world wherein all human beings might move freely, and without an escape hatch, I see an image of us fully actualized, on even ground. Our plans to move across expansive territory are met with smiles or indif-ference, or others' tales of the transformative, healing capacity of open space.

It is another morbidly hot August evening, years later. I am loading only the essentials—water, a change of clothes, my toothbrush—into my 1995 hatchback, whose engine may or may not survive the next 1,500 miles. I coast onto 10 East; I will take this road door-to-door from Los Angeles to Houston, where my oldest friend and the godson I have not yet met live. I drive at night, through the night. My visit is a surprise. No one has been told of my whereabouts, my destination, my planned trajectory through the Southwest.

The vastness of the Arizona desert overwhelms me, even in darkness. I feel the magnitude of my existence as though I am here and safely invisible all at once, exempted from the rules of rote responsibility and the mundane. I feel enormous.

I approach the Coronado National Forest, where the signage signifies campsites and motels ahead. I forgo both and pop my hatchback. With my headlamps on I scan for bear tracks, prop up my pillows, and rest my head on the edge of the bumper, listening to the electric hum of an occasional passing rig in the distance. I smoke a cigarette, because these are the occasions that draw out the romantic in me. I drift into sleep soundly, awakened by the heat and the orange glow of sun on the crests of the Santa Catalina Mountains. Their beauty immobilizes me. I want to sit longer, but the heat will climb rapidly, so I begin to reorganize the car for its next leg.

I arrive in El Paso before noon. The late morning sky is unfettered by the intrusion of industrial civilization and man-made light. I park and cross the Paso del Norte Bridge on foot. The massive span teems with fresh faces spilling out into the recently dedicated Leticia Chavarria Park in Ciudad Juarez, spanning both sides of the border, connecting friends and loved ones on the ground. I eat my lunch and fall asleep in the sun.

It will be later, mesmerized by the road and drifting deeper into the desert, that I am struck by the beauty of this city, once awash in viciousness, reclaimed through the heroism and sacrifice of some women who are doctors, lawyers, and journalists, and many more who are mothers, sisters, daughters, and exiled activists and workers in the maquiladoras. I am reminded of my own new world, one in which I no longer measure every step toward the horizon as a step away from my relative safety, a space where I am accounted for. I am struck that I no longer ask myself if the magnificence that lays ahead is worth it—meaning worth being (presumably) the last thing I ever see, or what I see last before being irrevocably altered.

This is still fiction. I can easily summon the audacity to make the trip, but the severity of the caveats, preparation, and adrenaline quickly erases the stillness that is the bedrock of my motivation. At every stage of imagining this simple narrative of driving through three states on my own terms, I cannot help but downshift into the escape hatch—to imagine my would-be attacker, imagine fending him off: the highway patrolman who pulls me over as I drive through the night; the tow-truck driver working the night shift; the serial rapist who sees me lying alongside my car while I identify constellations; the drunken teenage boys who approach me on my solo hike into the Grand Canyon. The specter of violence that haunts the border from every angle.

Utopias are hard-won. The writer and self-identified former teenage runaway Vanesssa Vaselka has written at length on the nuances of female travel, deftly connecting the danger in being a woman on the road with the absence of traveling female heroines in popular culture.

Our desire to move freely demands we operate with defiance, to occupy space in the same ways in which all of our gains as women have been made. This is not simple, but the only way. Throughout history, targeted people have gained power solely by resisting. Our vote, our position at the ballot box, something now so normalized we oft forget, was given only to white men. For the rest of us, there was only incredible physical risk for our place in line.

Thus, it is our visibility, solo in open space, that will both embolden and protect us. For our female Shangri-la to manifest, we must meet the trail. To rid it of vultures, we must claim it. Like Kathrine Switzer's 1967 attack by a race organizer for daring to compete in the Boston Marathon (the first woman to do so), the absurdity of a "woman's place" can only be eroded and redefined by her visibility.

It's sunset, and the final leg of my Houston trip. I am screwing the gas cap on my tank at a Love's outside San Antonio when I clock a figure staring at me, backlit at the parking lot's periphery. Without my glasses I can only see boots and short, spiky hair. I pop the fuel cover into place, glancing downward for my keys as the figure comes closer, and into focus. A hitchhiker. With the pink desert sky behind her, she looks like Tank Girl, Lori Petty's version. I open my passenger side door for her. We ease out of the parking lot, and with the sun behind us, onto the road.

Ria Fay-Berquist *is a writer, filmmaker, and educator, born during the fleeting cultural mutiny that came after disco, but before the crush of AIDS in San Francisco. She is currently a master's student and Urban Scholar at Harvard's Graduate School of Education, where she is exploring educational approaches for high-achieving kids in juvenile detention. Ria's nonfiction work has also appeared in* Gawker's *Sunday long-form series, curated by Kiese Laymon. She welcomes the conversation and quarantines the rabid on Twitter as @fayB.*

The Day without Body Shame

ERIN MATSON

You will get up in the morning. Your toes will fall on the floor with purpose. The noises of your body—the cracking joints, the yawns that sometimes turn into burps, the normal gas of a new day—if you notice them at all, they sound like an engine. You are just getting started.

Your mind may be pulling slowly out of a magical mauve fog, the kind tourists and artists would photograph if you were here for the purposes of display, which you are not. Your mind may be processing a dream, and no matter what it was, you are not ashamed of your ability to know, your ability to imagine, your physicality, and your spirituality.

To evaluate the body as separate from the mind is to evaluate the content of your character by the contours of shifting shadows.

The elevation of body and mind to a sacred space only you control is based in your inviolable right to take up space exactly as you are without judgment or guilt or evaluation or denigration. The mirror is a shiny piece of glass. The scale has numbers, but who gives a shit? You are so much more.

In a world without body shame, artifacts used to oppress women and girls begin to disappear or transition to a new purpose. Hair dryers can be tools for keeping warm. A collection of lipsticks can be used to create the finest oil paintings. Spanx can be used to slingshot a giggling child across the lawn.

In this world without body shame, you may still choose to wear lipstick and use beauty products, thank you very much. You may still choose to wear short skirts, or long skirts, or leggings. Objects and trappings do not define who you are. They are valid choices. They are, however, not compulsory. You can wear your hair short or nappy or long, and what people see is you. You don't need a tightening cream; you wear your cellulite and dance!

Once you've made your way out the door, nasty presumptions about your sexual life based on the shape of your body are exchanged for recognition of your humanity. Remember those dudes catcalling on the street? They have literally become cats (there is always room for more cats). Or, better yet, they will have stopped calling and started respecting. What you look like is not their business. How you love is not their business. No longer will anyone believe you have a sexual purpose that you have not declared for yourself. You understand your sexual purpose because you know it's yours to develop and own.

Your body will not be used to punish you for having more lines, more colors, more shapes than any one imagination can hold. You will not use your body to punish you. Others will not use your body to punish you. Your body, as crassly separated from your soul, is off limits. It is yours.

Your body is respected as the miracle that breathes, snores, smiles, cries, and brings you from the morning to the evening every day. For that, you love it without question. It is from this love of self that you experience an even greater love for others, a recognition that no body should be used to punish or disadvantage a person from within or without. Humanity is, on a physical level, a kaleidoscope of bodies. Every time a new body enters this world, space is created for it just as it is, and that movement makes the existing shades and shapes all the more beautiful as they shimmy and shine.

Compliments like "you look great" become "you are great." The mirror, if you bother to look at it, has completely forgotten what a digitally altered woman looks like, because you are so beautiful. Yes, you. You always are.

Erin Matson *is a feminist writer and grassroots organizer. At various points in her career she has served as an editor at large for RH Reality Check, a vice president of the National Organization for Women, and an advertising creative. She is an anorexia survivor.*

Queer in Public

COURTNEY BAXTER

I've found them in subway cars, in subway stations, on street corners, in restaurants, and once in a cemetery.

They are brief moments of affection between same-sex couples, interlocked hands or a stolen kiss here or there, in public spaces. I started documenting these couples and their acts of expressed love as my own act of protest against a larger culture of hate and harassment. I take photographs of contemporary public same-sex affection to create a mosaic of a future, truly queer utopia. It's a world where two women in Montana can hold hands on a trail, or two men, married for ten years in Taos, New Mexico, can kiss each other goodbye on their way to work. It's one in which a culture of love overpowers one of fear and homophobia.

Courtney Baxter *is the chief of staff at the OpEd Project. She graduated from Denison University with a BA in gender studies and international studies. Her work has been published in the* New York Times *and she is the creator of the website* Queer in Public.

The Free Girl Who Is Everything

JANET MOCK

The free girl with love being her birthright, liberation being her mission, and self-realization being her quest is my vision for an ideal society.

The free girl will walk down a crowded street in the daytime—unnoticed.

She will not feel obligated to shield herself with sunglasses or earbuds or cosmetics. She will not fret about her height or the space her frizzy curls occupy or how her lengthy thighs remain close. Like Celie and Nettie, they're sisters, refusing to part. She will be assured in the *is*ness of her stature, her presence, her being.

No one will speak to her unless she knows, respects, and trusts them. No one will squeeze her arm. No one will follow her with their lustful, their questioning, their spiteful gaze. She will not have to endure the whispers that greeted Janie upon her return to Eatonville. No one will call her out of her name, her identity, or her body.

She will exist without event, without harassment, without struggle.

The mundane, once considered a luxury for girls like her, will no longer be unattainable. An overwhelming sense of safety and communal support will be her default. She will not be left to fend for herself, pull herself up from the bootstraps, make something out of nothing. She will not have to crowdfund or go underground or seek resources in a man's lap to make ends meet. Her daily access needs—medicine, food, education, clothing, and shelter—will be a given.

Desperation will no longer be her driving force. Achieving survival will no longer be her quest. She will journey toward creativity and contentment and love.

Love will be the foundation of her relationships, providing her with affirmation and validation. She will believe she is deserving and worthy. She will believe she can dream, pursue, and achieve. She will believe she is entitled to all things, welcomed into all spaces, and free to define herself. When she declares who she is, everyone will nod.

In her world, the words "girls" and "women" do not need qualifiers. She will not furrow her brow wondering if her interlocking identities are ingrained in its definition. Because of her foremothers—Sylvia and Audre, Barbara and Marsha—she will no longer be burdened by the question Sojourner Truth had to ask: "Ain't I a woman?" When she hears "girls" and "women," Marissa Alexander, Gwen Araujo, Renisha McBride, CeCe

McDonald, Islan Nettles, Zoraida Reyes, her sisters in Nigeria, are all included. She will never doubt their inclusion, or hers.

She is not merely included; she is actually centered. She is centered because there are no gatekeepers to womanhood. It belongs to her, and no one can police her out. She is centered because solidarity is an act, not a label. She will never tiptoe toward sisterhood. She is centered because our feminism is solidly built on the belief that our freedom lies in her being free. And she will expect nothing less from us because she is everything.

This free girl is our liberation.

Janet Mock *is the author of the* New York Times *best seller* Redefining Realness *and a prominent advocate for trans women's rights. She's a board member at the Arcus Foundation and a contributing editor for* Marie Claire. *You can follow her on Twitter @JanetMock.*

When God Becomes a Woman

ABIGAIL CARNEY

most people do not notice.

One girl with her hands folded
kneels beside her bed.

A woman priest and a man priest say she instead of he
on Sunday.
A priest marries his daughter to a woman.
No one apologizes.

The articles drop out of the Bible
like swollen fruit.

It would be jarring to replace all the *he*s with *she*s
or worse with *its* or *he/she*s.
So God is only God.
God resting on all the work of creating God had done,
a proud bird upon its nest.

Abigail Carney *is a writer from Ohio. Her plays have been produced at the Secret Theatre, the Young Playwrights Festival, NYC Fringe, the Yale Playwrights' Festival, the New School for Drama, and in Sitka, Alaska.*

Seven Rituals from the Feminist Utopia
Prebirth to Postdeath

YUMI SAKUGAWA

Yumi Sakugawa *is an Ignatz Award–nominated comic book artist and the author of* I Think I Am in Friend-Love with You *and* Your Illustrated Guide to Becoming One with the Universe. *Her comics have also appeared in* Bitch, *the* Best American Nonrequired Reading 2014, *the* Rumpus, *the* Believer, *and other publications. A graduate of the fine art program of University of California, Los Angeles, she lives in Los Angeles.*

7 RITUALS FROM THE FEMINIST UTOPIA

PREBIRTH TO POSTDEATH

BY YUMI SAKUGAWA

YUMI SAKUGAWA

Interview with Harsh Crowd

The following is excerpted from an interview an editor conducted in person on October 11, 2014, with Rihana Abdulrashid-Davis, Willow Bennison, Dea Brogaard-Thompson, and Lena Faske—the members of Harsh Crowd, an all-female rock band of twelve-year-olds. Making waves straight out of the gate, Harsh Crowd has charmed audiences at venues such as Joe's Pub, the Frieze Art Fair and Madison Square Garden. The group formed at the Willie Mae Rock Camp for Girls and practice every weekish with their band coach, Caryn Havlik.

Okay! Is it okay with you all if I record this conversation?

Willow Bennison: You brought us doughnuts. You can do anything you want.

Good! So my first question is, how would you describe the sound of Harsh Crowd?

Bennison: We sound like Coldplay.

Caryn Havlik: You guys sound *way* better than Coldplay.

Dea Brogaard-Thompson: I'd say rock mixed with punk.

Lena Faske: It's also kinda poppy and jumpy.

Who are some of your rock idols?

Faske: Joan Jett. Le Tigre.

Bennison: The Orwells.

Faske: But that's a new one so…

Brogaard-Thompson: I feel like we find ourselves covering more bands.

Bennison: Yeah, more bands than single artists.

Brogaard-Thompson: Yeah, it's all bands.

Bennison: Yeah, 'cause *we're* a band.

I want to know, when you play music, how do you feel? I know that's kind of an abstract question.

Brogaard-Thompson: Well I'd have to use an adjective—

Use it!

Brogaard-Thompson: Empowered.

Rhianna Abdulrashid-Davis: Free. I feel happy and free playing through all the chords.

Faske: I definitely feel free. Like in my mind all my problems go away. A lot of times I also take my problems out on songs, and I write about my problems so then when I sing them or play them, it feels good to get it out.

Drums are good for that.

Faske: Yeah if I'm mad, I definitely won't, like, punch something—I'll get it out on the drums, you know.

Bennison: I can't think about anything else because you put all of yourself into the music.

Wow. Is there any other place that you feel that way?

Abdulrashid-Davis: My bedroom.

Faske: Listening to music. Anything with music basically!

This is basically what the Feminist Utopia Project is about. We're trying to imagine how the world would change if everyone—especially every girl—felt this way all the time.

[*An eruption of laughter*]

Bennison: The world would be so much better . . .

Brogaard-Thompson: I think about this all the time with my friends, I'm like, "If only you were in a band." [*Sighs*] "If only you knew."

Yes! Say more about that! How would your friends at school be different say, if they were all in their own bands?

Abdulrashid-Davis: They'd be less violent.
Brogaard-Thompson: People would find out, "Oh, I can release all this stuff into music, then maybe I wouldn't be so angry all the time."
Faske: Our songs bring out our personalities and our taste in music, too. I'd hear everyone else's way of writing a song and I would actually get to know them a lot better. My friends could learn that music is a way to make you feel better—that it's a way to let out all of your feelings without keeping them locked inside.

Is there anything that feels unfair to you about the rock world that you would want to be different in a feminist utopia?

Bennison: Guy bands get so much more coverage.
Faske: Girl bands are called girl bands. And we hate that! Because it doesn't matter! If you're a girl or a boy, you're making music—you don't have to call it a girl band or a boy band! I don't want to have to pick sides either—I'm not on the girl band side or the boy band side.

Bennison: I'm on the music side! "Girl band" is more than just a label that has to do with gender—it's also a type of sound—and it's not a sound that we want to have, or that we do have. So when people call us a girl band . . . it's like . . . *well* . . . we're *not a girl band.*

Faske: Yeah, we are a group of four girls playing music, but we're not a girl band! And sometimes people even say, "Oh, you're good for kids," and "You're good for a girl band"—but that's not even a compliment to us because saying "good for a . . . " shouldn't be [a compliment].

Well you guys played the best cover of "Deceptacon" that I have ever heard. That was amazing. I want to ask you guys more about the future. What do you want the future of rock to be? Do you guys see yourselves in it?

Faske: I'm definitely going to be in rock forever. I've already outlasted all of my friends trying to turn me to the dark side . . . of Auto-Tune.

[Laughter]

Bennison: People on Auto-Tune are *so* talented.
Faske: Yeah!
Bennison: No, it's machines being talented!

[*In a robot voice*] It is robot music.

[No one laughs]

Okay! Continuing to think about the future . . . what do you want to do when you "grow up"?

Abdulrashid-Davis: I want to be a musician, an artist, a doctor, and a writer.

Brogaard-Thompson: I definitely see myself playing guitar for the rest of my life. I'll probably laugh at myself in twenty years, but at this moment I can't imagine anything else. I definitely plan on being a musician.

Faske: I want to continue being in a band and my job to be something involved in music. Maybe a music producer or supervisor. Anything with music. I love music. I already am auditioning for music high schools and hopefully music college.

Bennison: I always pictured myself more on Broadway than doing rock music. But I can see myself doing this!

Last question: are you guys accepting new members? New members who are . . . twenty-four years old?

[*Laughter*]

Bennison: Well, you could be a lighting designer.

Brogaard-Thompson: Yeah, you could be a roadie?

Abdulrashid-Davis: You could be a fan!

Appendix A:
Imperfect Categories

The pieces in this collection don't fit into neat boxes—that's why we haven't arranged the anthology into chapters. However, we've done our best to point out a few porous and overlapping categories that may help you navigate this book.

The Body:

Labor and Economic Justice:

Our Myths and Narratives:

Racial Justice:

Parenting and Family:

Education:

Trans Justice:

Language:

Love and Relationships:

Organizing:

Health Care:

Disability Rights:

Queer Rights:

Interviews:

Fiction:

Visual Contributions:

If You're in the Mood for Laughing:

If You're in the Mood for Beyoncé:

Appendix B:
Sightings of Utopia

While putting together this book, the editors enjoyed texting one another each time they stumbled across utopia-related signage. Please enjoy this sampling from their collection!

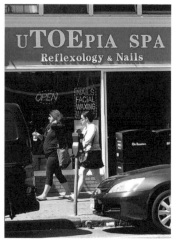